# BETWEEN GOD AND MAN

D1594624

*Pope Innocent III*

# BETWEEN GOD AND MAN

Six Sermons on the Priestly Office

---

*Translated with an Introduction by*
*Corinne J. Vause and †Frank C. Gardiner*
*and a Foreword by James M. Powell*

*The Catholic University of America Press*
*Washington, D.C.*

Copyright © 2004
The Catholic University of America Press

*Library of Congress Cataloging-in-Publication Data*
Innocent III, Pope, 1160 or 61-1216.
    [Sermones de diversis. English]
    Between God and man : six sermons on the priestly office /
translated with an introduction by Corinne J. Vause and Frank C.
Gardiner ; and a foreword by James M. Powell.— 1st ed.
    p. cm. — (Medieval texts in translation)
    Includes bibliographical references and index.
    ISBN 0-8132-1365-7 (pbk. : alk. paper)
    1. Clergy—Office—Sermons—Early works to 1800.
2. Catholic Church—Sermons—Early works to 1800.
3. Sermons, Latin—Early works to 1800.   4. Sermons, Latin—
Translations into English.   I. Vause, Corinne J., 1931–
II. Gardiner, F. C.   III. Title.   IV. Series.
BV662.I5613 2004
262'.142—dc21
                                                2003011990

# CONTENTS

# FOREWORD

*James M. Powell*

The study of the role of preaching is central to an understanding of the nature of the church.[1] The New Testament makes clear that preaching occupied an important place in the creation of the church. While there are numerous mentions and even summaries of preaching in the Gospels, the Acts of the Apostles, and the Epistles, the liturgical and sacramental aspect of the church received much less attention in these sources. Yet it was precisely this sacramental and liturgical church that emerged most clearly in the fourth century, after the grant of toleration by the Emperor Constantine. For a long time, there was a tendency to criticize the Middle Ages for this emphasis and its seeming neglect of preaching, particularly during the intense debates over religion in the Reformation and post-Reformation periods. Protestants sought precedents for their preaching in the primitive church and identified with heretical groups like the Waldensians or the Lollards, who were known for their preaching. The opposition of the church to their preaching was seen as confirmation of Protestant criticism. Yet, this view ignored the vital preaching tradition in the medieval church especially after the mid-eleventh century.[2]

From the earliest Christian centuries, clergy and laity had found it necessary to adapt to changing situations thrust on them by the instability of the late antique and early medieval Roman world. We know too little about the changes that occurred as the church moved from Roman audiences to those composed of Germanic barbarians. What we do know suggests efforts to reach out more effectively to an uneducated audience. The numerous initiatives of missionaries from Ireland to continental Europe pointed the way for new approaches to evangelization. Conversion was at first directed at the leaders of the Germanic tribes rather than at the masses. The conversion of the latter was the work of a gradually formed local clergy, both monastic and secular, who sought to communicate the fundamentals of Christianity in images and metaphors, often in poetic and alliterative terms that could be retained in memory and thus entered into the cultural savings accounts that were slowly being amassed in the period from the seventh through the tenth centuries. Of the preaching of this period, we have only those survivals that were the most valued exemplars.[3]

By the early eleventh century, the process of evangelization had begun to reach even into the backwaters and to produce unique individuals committed to the kind of monastic spirituality that sprang from an intense individual experience. They found their inspiration in early monastic and eremetical experience, but they were addressing concerns that were part of their own age. Expanding population and increased prosperity, based largely on income from agriculture, made it possible and even imperative to focus on solutions to societal problems. Monasticism inspired many of those seeking a better way.[4] John Gualbert, Dominic of Sora, Robert of Arbrissel, to name a few, were important to a revival of preaching that reached beyond the boundaries between the monastery and the world.[5] One important characteristic of this period was the formation of new kinds of religious communities. The range of such activity, from the foundation of the Cistercians and the Premonstratensians to cathedral canonries and lay confraternities, reached a large segment of society. The greatest preacher of the age was a Cistercian, Bernard of Clairvaux. During this same period, the crusade provided another stimulus to preaching. Pope Urban II himself had begun by preaching the crusade at the Council of Clermont in 1095.[6] Increasingly, this new religiosity was directed toward remaking the world into a kind of ideal monastic community. The potential of this transformation for solving the problems of a world beset by violence and poverty was grasped by such popular figures as Peter Valdes and Arnold of Brescia. Their extremism ought not blind us to the strong ties between their message and that of the reformers. They were not unique in their emphasis on preaching. Their voices are often difficult to distinguish from others whose orthodoxy was never challenged.

From the mid-eleventh century and even earlier in some cases, cathedral and monastic schools had been important centers for the education of preachers. These schools were repositories of studies in grammar and rhetoric, based upon both classical and Carolingian sources. In the second half of the twelfth century, the first universities were developing in Bologna and Paris. These centers attracted students from all over western Europe. We should not, however, regard the education offered in the twelfth-century universities as contrasting sharply with that offered in the cathedral and monastic schools. Certainly, education was becoming more formalized, but the content changed rather gradually.[7] Those who studied in Paris and Bologna were, therefore, not separated by any deep chasm from the popular preachers of the earlier part of the century. Fulk of Neuilly, Oliver of Paderborn, and James of Vitry, all of whom had frequented the schools of Paris, were notable popular preachers, whose words reflected the religious currents of the day and the concerns of contemporary society.

Pope Innocent III was a contemporary of these and other preachers in Paris and Bologna. As Cardinal Lothar, he not only studied in the schools, but authored a number of theological treatises. While scholars have usually hastened to deny his work originality, his contemporaries regarded it as a valuable contribution. In fact, his election to the papacy at the young age of thirty-seven was probably connected directly to his reputation as an author. When we examine these treatises, we are struck by their pastoral character.

Their author had little interest in the academic debates that occupied the masters in the schools. That is not to say that he was unaware of such matters. He was certainly capable of picking his way through contemporary theological debates, such as that over the Trinity or the presence of Christ in the Eucharist, but his emphasis was not on differences in doctrine so much as it was on faith as the basis for the Christian way of life. Still, his approach was very much that of the schools, and the content of his thought reflected such masters as Peter of Corbie and Peter Chanter. Throughout his writings, he combined the ability to utilize dramatic imagery in order to serve practical ends.

Papal sermon collections were rare in the early middle ages. We know that popes preached at synods and that Urban II had preached often to promote the crusade. Yet we possess few of these sermons. For this reason, it is remarkable that both Innocent III and his successor Pope Honorius III compiled their sermons in collections.[8] Moreover, this was not accidental. Innocent had sent a copy of his collection to Abbot Arnald of Citeaux. Honorius provided copies not only to the Cistercians, but also to the Dominicans and the Archpriest of Santa Maria Maggiore, where he had been a canon. In Innocent's case, he responded to a request from Arnald made at the behest of his chaplain, Nicholas, a Cistercian of that abbey. Honorius acted on his own initiative for reasons that reveal a desire on his part to "improve" on Innocent's collection.

There can be little doubt that Innocent's sermons were motivated by the same goals that led him to write his various theological treatises. He was a product of the schools and wanted to share his learning with his colleagues and the members of the Roman clergy. His approach is didactic, as befitted his education. Innocent delivered at least some of his sermons in the vernacular; Honorius III composed his sermons in the vernacular and delivered them prior to becoming pope.[9] After his accession to the papacy, he translated them into Latin and revised them for presentation. His purpose was also didactic, but his concerns were rather different, more pastoral even than Innocent's. He also seems to have been concerned to provide more authorities for his interpretations. This suggests that he differed from Innocent, and perhaps also with his Parisian views, preferring a more traditional approach.

The sermons translated here were preached on special occasions and under special circumstances. They were not part of the collection that Innocent sent to the Cistercians. Although modern historians have studied them as exemplars of Innocent's thought, they have not, as a rule, looked at them in the context of the events and circumstances that led to their production. Thus, traditional *topoi*, such as the corruption of the clergy, which were completely understandable when addressed to the clergy gathered in synod to listen to their bishop, could easily become the basis for historical generalizations regarding the state of the clergy in Rome. This is not to argue that there is no validity to these strictures, but that they cannot be generalized beyond the circumstances that surrounded them. Much more could be written about other themes found in these sermons, but the present state of research does not permit conclusions. Suffice it to say, the value of reading these sermons in translation rests not with their value as complete statements of the situation of the church in the early thirteenth century, but of the important access they provide to the thinking of the pope on specific occasions.

Innocent III was a transitional figure in the history of the medieval papacy. He reigned at a time when the church was confronted with myriad problems, from concerns over heresy to the evangelization of northern lands and the promotion of the crusade. Innocent was a champion of reform. Like his predecessors, he perceived reform first and foremost as a strengthening of the institutional church and of clerical discipline. But the church of his day was changing very rapidly as the laity were searching for a spirituality suited to their individual needs. These sermons present only a part of a very complex picture in which Innocent attempted to mediate differing visions of reform. His pontificate was under constant strain and, at times, he was unsuccessful or even temporarily lost his way. If that aspect does not come through clearly in these sermons, its absence does not detract from their value. Rather, it demonstrates the difficult task of the historian.

# INTRODUCTION

"Among the many ministries that belong to the pastoral office, the virtue of holy preaching is the most excellent."[1] Thus the brilliant and controversial Pope Innocent III proclaimed what he believed to be the highest priority among his duties as chief shepherd of Christendom. Considering the vast scope of his papal accomplishments, his work as a preacher may seem less significant than his more secular concerns. Yet, the great number of sermons he did indeed write and deliver during his intensely active and often contentious career, is testimony to the value he placed on his vocation as a preacher. Before Innocent's time only Leo I (440–61) and Gregory I (590–604), also men deeply engaged in administrative and secular affairs, had left such extensive homiletic legacies. A study of Innocent's sermons confirms his reputation as a learned and eloquent scholar, exegete, and theologian. It also shows him to have been an astute psychologist, as well as a priest fully engaged in the realities of active ministry. His preaching, in the assessment of a modern critic, "articulated a role for the papacy that was watchman, spiritual and religious leader, and active reformer."[2]

## Historical and Biographical Background

Although Innocent's pontificate (1198–1216) was to become the zenith of the medieval papacy, on the day of his election, January 8, 1198, he found himself in charge of a vast and unruly flock. He had inherited from his predecessors a church torn by heresy and schism and, as has often been the case throughout its history, in need of reform. Christendom itself was in disorder, disrupted by political turmoil within and threatened by Muslims abroad. Rather than be dismayed by these difficulties, the new Pope was apparently eager to take on "the existential problems with which the church and Christendom were wrestling in his day, and he was burning to be able to contribute to their effective solution."[3] During the eighteen years of his papacy he would confront all these problems, and in so doing, strengthen the papal monarchy in relation to secular authority, and define Christian society in its relationships with contemporary heretics, with the Jewish community, and with Islam. Given the controversial nature of the challenges he faced, Innocent's record in dealing with them continues to be a subject of debate.[4] Whatever judgment history may give to this great Pope's actions, however, there can be no doubt that he devoted himself tirelessly to devising solutions to the problems he perceived as the responsibility of the papal office.

When taking on the daunting task of reforming the church itself, Innocent directly confronted the deficiencies and delinquencies of the clergy, the corps of bishops, priests, and deacons who held responsibility for serving the religious needs of humanity. In general this group was badly in need of rehabilitation and revitalization. The specific steps necessary for bringing about this clerical reform would be codified in the documents of the Fourth Lateran Council. In this collection of *Sermones de diversis* Innocent anticipates those reforms, speaking directly to those in Holy Orders who, like himself, had been anointed as preachers of the Gospel and ministers of the sacraments. Here we see the chief shepherd carrying out his pastoral work by shepherding the pastors themselves. These sermons are therefore "meta-pastoral," in that they teach the pastoral role even as they are the means Innocent employs for carrying out that role. Innocent addresses the clergy as his "sons and brothers," as he unfolds for them his vision of their shared priestly vocation.

The man himself, Giovanni Lothario dei Conti of Segni (1160–1216), who was to become Pope Innocent III, was a Roman by birth and inheritance. His family was wealthy and influential, and Pope Clement III was his uncle. He grew up well acquainted with both the political and religious intrigues of the city of Rome. He left Rome for his advanced education, which began in Paris, known for its theological and philosophical curriculum. There Innocent may have been among the group of students who gathered around the famous master Peter the Chanter.[5] After leaving Paris, Innocent took up further study at Bologna, which was noted for its curriculum in both canon and civil law. It was there that he was ordained a deacon. Although there is some doubt that Innocent actually received a degree as a canon lawyer,[6] as pontiff he held consistories three times a week to which students of the law would flock in order to improve their education by observing his handling of cases.[7]

Upon his return to Rome, probably in 1189, Lothario appears to have gone immediately into the Curia,[8] where he served during the pontificates of Clement III (1187–91) and Celestine III (1191–98). In acknowledgment of the quality of his work he was advanced to the rank of cardinal-deacon, but was not ordained to the priesthood until after his election as Pope. As cardinal he administered the Church of Sts. Sergius and Bacchus, which lay within the Forum at the Arch of Septimius Severus.[9] He also wrote three theological treatises: *De miseria condicionis humanae* (also known as *De contemptu mundi*), or *Concerning the Misery of the Human Condition; De missarum mysteriis* (also known as *De sacro alteris mysterio*), or *Concerning the Sacred Mystery of the Altar* [the Mass]; and *De quadripartita specie nuptiarum*, or *Concerning the Four Kinds of Marriage*.[10] The *De miseria* became a very popular book, surviving in almost seven hundred manuscripts, and *De mysteriis*, an expression of Innocent's very deep Eucharistic piety, was absorbed into a standard liturgical textbook of the later Middle Ages.[11]

When Lothario of Segni became Pope Innocent III, he was thirty-seven-years-old, young, in the eyes of his contemporaries, for the responsibility he was assuming. His anonymous biographer says that he was elected because of "the honesty of his morals and his knowledge of letters."[12] Despite his wealth he lived simply, and there was never a suggestion of any impropriety in his private life. Although a man of slight stature, he had a dynamism that belied the fragile health that plagued him throughout his life. He is further described as "comely,"[13] with a sonorous voice, a strong personality,[14] a man of great courage and self-control.[15] In sum, Lothario Segni was a man uniquely gifted for his time and place in history: a very well-educated aristocrat, an experienced administrator, and, according to his own testimony, a man of the very greatest faith.[16] As Pope Innocent III he was prepared to turn all his talents and all the powers of his papal office toward solving the problems of his world and times.

## Homiletic Background

When Innocent III took up his work as a preacher, the Christian preaching tradition was already thirteen hundred years old. Christ himself, and John the Baptist before him, had been preachers of the Gospel, and Christ's last words to his followers were, "Preach the Gospel to all creatures."[17] According to the Acts of the Apostles, the first preaching of the Gospel was inspired by the Holy Spirit.[18] Many of the preachers had no formal training, relying on the persuasive power of their message, rather than on their own oratorical skills. Others, such as Paul, were well-educated converts who had been trained in classical rhetoric, and could now put that training to use in spreading their new religion. Among the most famous of these converts was Augustine of Hippo (354–430), a professional rhetorician, whose treatise *De doctrina Christiana* set the standards for a Christian rhetoric. The common practice among early Christians, however, was for preaching to be done as an informal homily, deliberately simple and non-structured, a conversation among the faithful, not an oratorical discourse.[19]

Missionary activity continued to spread the Gospel across Europe in the following centuries, although preaching was not the only means for communicating the Christian message. Often conversion was set in motion by personal contact rather than by public instruction. Sometimes a barbarian chieftain, converted through the importuning of his Christian wife, would command that all his people be baptized.[20] Some holy preachers accomplished conversions by stunning their audiences with miracles, rather than by reasoned argument.[21] The practical realities of life in early medieval Europe, difficulties in travel, frequent wars and invasions, often made it impossible for congregations to assemble, particularly in rural areas, so that the giving of formal sermons became a principal interest of monks rather than of the secular clergy. Nevertheless, these troubled centuries produced preachers of splendid talent and far-reaching renown: Ambrose (d. 397), a contemporary of Augustine; Leo the Great (d. 461); Gregory the Great (540–604): Aelfric (955–1020); Wulfstan (d. 1023); and Anselm (1032–1109), among others. Yet, it would be with the advent of the High Middle Ages, the development of the universities, and the rise of heresy that public preaching would take on new value, become an important field of study, and emerge as a strong influence in the affairs of the time.

The university setting of the twelfth century produced a distinctive style of preaching based on an academic model. Peter the Chanter (d. 1197) had identified the work of the teaching master as having three parts: *lectio, disputatio, praedicatio:* lecturing, disputing, and preaching.[22] The material for all three activities was drawn from Scripture. Lecturing was a detailed, word-by-word analysis of the sacred page. Disputation, as the name implies, was the pro and con discussion of obscure and disputed passages. Preaching was the natural outgrowth of this intensive Scriptural study. All the scholars had been trained in rhetoric as part of the Liberal Arts curriculum, based on the Ciceronian tradition inherited from the classical world. At the end of the twelfth century there were, how-

ever, few textbooks on sermonizing available to the student preacher. The *Pastoral Care* of Gregory the Great was still popular. Rabanus Maurus had written *De institutione clericorum* in the ninth century, and Guibert of Nogent's *Liber quo ordine sermo fieri debeat* had
been written in the eleventh century.[23] One of Innocent's contemporaries, Alan of Lille, a Cistercian, had written *Summa de arte praedicatoria* in about 1199,[24] and the influence of Alan's work can be
found in Innocent's sermons. Despite the paucity of training man-
uals in the twelfth century, every master was expected to be a
preacher, and the delivery of an inception sermon became one of
the qualifications for the Master's degree. It was from the ranks of
these university masters, the scholastics, that many great preachers,
Innocent III among them, would come.

During the same time that the scholastics were honing their
homiletic skills in the classroom, another category of preachers
was gaining popularity among the people. These were the inspired
laymen, often itinerant and mendicant, who were appealing to the
common people with their messages of moral reform. Although
some of the lay preachers, such as Peter Waldo (d. c. 1205–15), were
labeled heretics by the church, others such as the Humiliati, and
later St. Francis, were allowed to preach moral reform, and to live
lives of evangelical poverty. Innocent's acknowledgment of these
humble preachers illustrated his understanding of their place in his
own work of reform. It was within this setting, of intense scholastic training in discourse on the one hand, and a thirst for simple
spiritual nourishment on the other, that Innocent would spend his
own preaching career.

The rise of heresy became a prime factor in inspiring a renewed
interest in preaching. The heresy that was spreading rapidly
through Europe in the twelfth century was Catharism, a form of
religious dualism, known also as Albigensianism because one of its
strongholds was the city of Albi in southern France. The Cathars'
dualistic belief held that spiritual creation is good, but material
things including human bodies are evil. Inherent in Albigensianism

is the denial of the doctrine of the Incarnation, that Christ's divine nature was conjoined fully with human nature, the doctrine upon which the whole notion of the Redemption relies. The heresy was, therefore, in direct opposition to centuries of Catholic teaching which maintained that Christ, God himself, has a human body in which he lived his earthly life, suffered a real and painful death, and is now living resurrected in heaven. The Cathars' practical application of this detestation of matter meant denial of the efficacy of the sacraments, an abhorrence of marriage because it produces more human bodies, and extreme mortification of the body, sometimes to the point of suicide. One of the most significant characteristics of the Cathar heresy was its elitism, by which it "reserved the full Christian life in this world to the dedicated few,"[25] a notion foreign to the Catholic Church's definition of itself as "universal." Much of the appeal of Catharism lay in the apparent purity of life of its adherents, which contrasted with the moral laxity often found among the orthodox clergy.

At the height of its popularity, Catharism, or Albigensianism, attracted the support of powerful political leaders who furthered their own territorial interests by joining forces with heretical bishops in defiance of those political rulers who adhered to the traditional Catholic doctrine. Innocent first sought to convert the heretics with a preaching campaign, commissioning the Cistercians to undertake this spiritual crusade. Later, when the Cistercians were not able to carry it through, he gave the new Order of Preachers, the "Dominicans," informal permission to undertake it. The preaching effort, although it had some success, could not uproot the widespread heresy which was more than merely a disagreement among simple believers on both sides. The stakes in the struggle included secular concerns that were so entangled with the religious controversy that preaching alone could not counteract the political pressures that were fueling the dispute. The result of the conflict was a bitterly harsh and protracted war, known now as the Albigensian Crusade. This crusade, which lasted beyond Innocent's time, finally accomplished its goal of crushing the heresy, but at great cost in human suffering and territorial damage.[26] Nevertheless, it was always Innocent's desire to convert rather than to punish the heretics.[27] He recognized that it was the Cathars' desire for sanctity and for living the apostolic life that made their beliefs attractive, while rendering them ripe for extremism.

The increased interest in preaching that grew out of university study, and was fed by the need to address heresy, would produce, in the early years of the thirteenth century, a number of homiletic treatises, and would even develop a new sermon genre, the "university" or "thematic" sermon, the first new rhetorical form since Cicero's time.[28] This was a highly formulaic and elaborately arranged discourse that required a great deal of skill to compose. Although its development was occurring during Innocent's lifetime, it does not appear to have been an influential part of his scholastic training. Frederick Imkamp has done an analysis of Innocent's Lateran IV sermon using the "university" sermon as his analytical tool.[29] Although Imkamp's work can increase appreciation of the sermon, the parallel with the "university" model is awkward to establish, and not convincing. The structure of the "university" sermon as described by Thomas of Salisbury is noticeably different from Innocent's sermon form.[30] The protheme, for example, and the opening prayer—identifying features of the thematic scheme—are never used by Innocent; nor were his divisions of the sermon sections as elaborately and formulaically balanced as the "university" model would prescribe.

Among his other impressive talents, Innocent's skill as a preacher is outstanding. His charismatic personality, his prodigious memory, and his sonorous voice gave him a natural flair for public speaking. His scholastic and legal training supplied him with intellectual tools for precise and dynamic expression. His mastery of homiletic techniques is evident in the variety of organizational schemes he employed. Not one of the *De diversis* sermons has the same form as another, yet each is perfectly crafted for its purpose, demonstrating his command of both traditional and contemporary methods. Added to these requisites was his conviction that preaching was a principal responsibility for him, as for all clergy, and one from which the other demands of his office could not exempt him. There is, of course, no certainty that all of these sermons were actually preached by Innocent III. Yet, the rhythm of the Latin phrasing, the vocal flow of the wording, the interjections which appear to be extemporaneous, the adaptation of the sermons to specific circumstances, and the tone of immediacy that can be felt in most of them, lead us to believe that they may very well have been spoken by Innocent himself on the occasions for which they were composed. It would not in any way diminish their value to us if we were to learn that the sermons had not been delivered to live audiences. Nevertheless, the reader may hope that indeed there were listeners present to hear these words from the Pope's own lips and in his own resonant voice.

## Major Themes

The primary theme of these sermons is the concept that the priest has been established as intermediary between God and mankind. The idea is, of course, not original with Innocent. John Chrysostom had stated the Christian sacerdotal tradition clearly in the fourth century: "The priest is in the midst, between God and men: he brings us the good things of God, and bears to him our prayers."[31] Innocent explains the idea of "being in the midst" more fully.

Priests are mediators between God and mankind, for they bring the divine precepts of God to the people by preaching, and carry the wishes of the people to God in supplicating. Priests must so exist that they may be both pleasing to God and be accepted by men. For as Pope Alexander says, "The worthier Christ's priests are, the more easily will they be heard in the needs of the people for whom they pray." And the Apostle, "He is the mediator not of just one' (Gal. 3:20). No one can reconcile discords,

who is not at the same time in accord with both sides in the bonds of association and of friendship. If he who displeases is sent to intercede, the
animosity of the irate is provoked to worse.[32]

Innocent found his prototype for the Christian clergy in the ancient Aaronide priesthood of Israel and the tribe of Levi, set apart
from the people and dedicated to the service of God and the of-
fering of sacrifice. Under the Christian discipline these sacerdotal
powers of mediation were transformed. Thus, in Innocent's view,
the sacrificial duties of Aaron and his sons prefigured the Eucharist, which is confected in the sacrifice of the Mass; Aaron's
duty to discern whether lepers had been cured of their fearsome
disease prefigured the judging of guilt and innocence in the sacramental forgiving of sins;[33] and, as God empowered Aaron to
"teach Jacob God's testimonies, and give Israel light on His Law,"[34]
so were Christian priests commissioned to teach sound doctrine.

As an extension of this model Innocent saw in the High Priest
of Israel the historical and symbolic prefiguration of the Pope, the
supreme pontiff.[35] As the successor to Peter, the Pope held the
"keys to the kingdom of heaven," and Peter's station at heaven's
gate was reminiscent of that held by the High Priest standing at
the "door of the tabernacle of testimony" (Lev. 4:4), the place of
theophany, of judgment and revelation between YHWH and his
people. Innocent believed that both pontiffs were to mediate between the eternal and the temporal, the ideal and the contingent,
the realms of the seen and the unseen, the absence and the presence of God. Much has been made of Innocent's claim that he was
"constituted mediator between God and mankind, below God but
higher than mankind; who judges all, and is judged by none."[36]
Given Innocent's understanding of the medial position of priest
and pontiff, this is indeed the very position in which the Pope, as
principal mediator, should be: as the constantly harrowed but essential mediator between God and mankind.

As the High Priest was appointed from the tribe of Levi, so the
bishop or the Pope is chosen from the presbyterium. This idea of

the priesthood as a brotherhood of clergy emerges as a sub-theme in the sermons. For Innocent, the bishop or the Pope is not an authority set over the clergy from outside, but one of their members who has been chosen from among them. When Innocent addresses his clergy he calls them "dearly loved sons and brothers."[37] Considering the care he gives to establishing the fraternal and corporate nature of the sacrament of Holy Orders, it rings true for him to invoke this familial relationship. Throughout his sermons he speaks as a member of this group, anointed as they were, and sharing their lot. This notion of the comradeship of the clergy is as strongly stressed in these sermons as is any notion of papal power, and mutual concern for the "care of the churches" is the repeated theme of these pastoral admonitions and challenges. Innocent would have agreed with the statement that the Pope cannot "think of himself as a lonely autocratic monarch," but rather as the ranking member of the priestly corps.[38] He is very clear on this point:

The name of "bishop" sounds more for labor (*oneris*) than for honor (*honoris*). "Episkopos" in Greek is translated "superintendent" in Latin, carrying the duties of overseer; as the Lord says, "Sons of men, I have given you an overseer of the House of Israel" (Ezek. 3:16–17), not that he might negligently direct the people committed to him, but that he might diligently watch out for them. Thus the Apostle said, "Whoever desires to be a bishop, desires a good work" (1 Tim. 3:1). He does not say "honor," but "work," for a bishop is elected not that he might command, but that he might bring benefits.[39]

Over and above the powers and obligations of priesthood and episcopacy shared with other clergy, Innocent, as Vicar of Christ, claimed a "plenitude of power" over the church,[40] a unique and universal jurisdiction that is another recurring theme in these sermons. The phrase *plenitudo potestatis* had its origin under Leo I (440–61), who linked it to the concept of *pars sollicitudinis*, a "share of the solicitude" by which the Pope and the bishops together participated in a sort of pastoral supervision and protection of the individual churches. What Innocent understood by the claim of "fullness of power" has generated extensive scholarly analysis and debate. In the last few decades scholars have arrived at a consensus that *plenitudo potestatis* is in Innocent's usage not only the Pope's full authority to make judgments on moral issues concerning the public as well as private decisions of secular rulers, but also the obligation to speak out on moral and spiritual issues.[41] Colin Morris succinctly summarizes this scholarly opinion:

> That to Innocent fullness of power (*plenitudo potestatis*) referred strictly to supreme spiritual authority, and that the claim of power over the whole world was also spiritual in content: it indicated universal authority in contrast with the restricted jurisdiction of all other prelates.[42]

And in a paraphrase of Innocent:

> Because all humans are sinful and need the intercession of priests, the priests, and in particular the Pope as the highest priest, could take disciplinary action against secular rulers who, because of their sinfulness (*ratione peccati*), have erred.[43]

Because the Pope, as Bishop of Rome, is considered to be the successor of Saint Peter, Innocent explains his position vis-à-vis other bishops in terms of Peter's status among the other Apostles. He finds that explanation in the "Petrine" texts of the Gospels: Matthew 16:18–19, Luke 22:31–32, and John 21:15–17. For him these are clear evidence that Christ had given Peter the "uniqueness of the one among and above the many, the Pope among the bishops."[44] To these traditional Petrine references Innocent's exegesis often added Hebrews 5:7, an assurance that Christ the High Priest's prayers are always heard because of his reverence for the Father. The application of this text to Luke 22:31–32, Christ's reference to his prayer that Peter persevere in his faith, is Innocent's own, which he claims not in "boundless self-confidence, but as [accepting] a divine challenge and an awesome responsibility."[45] Although the Pope is susceptible to personal sin, Innocent believes that he will not lose his faith, because Christ's High Priestly prayer for his fidelity will always be answered.

The figure of the Pope as a servant is also a recurring theme in these sermons. Sermon Two (Coronation) is based on the Biblical text of the faithful servant of the household (Mt. 24:45). However, more frequently quoted from that sermon is the text describing the work of the field servant of Jeremiah 1:10:

Behold, I have constituted you today over nations and kings, to root up, and pull down, and to lay waste, and to destroy, and to build, and to plant.

In context the agricultural figure is evident. When Innocent cites the text, he does so in the same sense as did Gregory the Great in explaining the work of preachers[46] and Bernard of Clairvaux in describing the papal office metaphorically as the work of a "sweating peasant."[47] In this sense the text had been prominent in papal letters and reformist writings from the time of Gregory VII, and through the twelfth century it was "a commonplace of the papal chancery, as a public expression of the papacy's pastoral mission in the Church."[48] The passage was glossed in detail in the *Glossa Ordinaria*, and later commented on by John of Paris (c. 1250–1306), as having "no relevance to the deposition and destruction of kings of earth and the creation of others in their place, but refers to the rooting out of vices and the planting of true faith and morals, in the sense of that passage of 1 Corinthians 3:9 'You are God's field, God's building.'"[49] For Innocent, the commissioning of Jeremiah explicitly parallels and prefigures the commissioning of Peter in Matthew 16:18–19:

I have constituted you over nations and kings. =
    You are Peter, and upon this rock I will build my church;
To root up and pull down, and build and plant. =
    Whatever you bind upon earth will be bound in heaven
    and whatever you loose upon earth will be loosed in heaven;
Be not afraid in their presence, for I am with you to deliver
    you. (Jer. 1:8) =
The gates of hell will not prevail against it.[50]

This conflating of the Petrine and Jeremiah passages clearly asserts the prophetic role of the papacy in the sense of "judging the times and events of history from the viewpoint of the sovereign design of God, which is a plan of rule and of salvation."[51] This spiritual duty of judgment, belonging to all bishops, was from at least the fifth century attributed particularly to the Bishop of Rome.[52] The Pope, then, was constituted to judge all, to be the intermediary between the law of God and the individual cases brought before him. Innocent was unremitting in this office.

## Conclusion

For Innocent and other medieval clergy the example for their preaching commission was Christ himself. "The Word [of God] was the mediator between God and men, whose redemption enabled them to know God and to bear God to each other in human words."[53] As Christ was Word of God in the flesh, so were the Scriptures the word of God on the sacred page. Preaching was the instrument for mediating the sacred page to the people. This group of sermons is Innocent's effort to model this mediation for his own clergy. With a sincerity that went beyond routine protestations of humility, Innocent often deplored the distractions of papal business that kept him from preaching as often as he thought he should. Nevertheless, it is noteworthy that the sermons are not touched by the political concerns that took so much of his time. They were mediations in the sense that they applied spiritual and moral principles to the individual situations of human life, and offered spiritual and moral solutions to the problems of the human condition. As chief pastor and pontiff Innocent III gave his clerical and episcopal brothers a wealth of practical and inspirational examples of homiletic excellence.

## Notes on the Text

The six sermons of Innocent III translated here are those grouped in Migne's Patrologia Latina (PL) as *Sermones de diversis*.[54] The selection of this set of sermons for study is valuable for two reasons. First, Sermons Two (Consecration) and Six (Lateran IV) mark the inauguration and culmination of Innocent's career as bishop and Pope. Taken together with Sermons Three and Four, these sermons present his essential vision of the papal constitution and its prerogatives. Moreover, all six sermons *De diversis* present Innocent's precise and pragmatic analysis of the sacrament of Holy Orders. Because the reformation of the clergy was at the heart of Innocent's plan for the reformation of the church, his instructions on the nature of priesthood give us a valuable key for understanding the attitudes he held when undertaking that reform.

Unlike Innocent's other sermons in Migne's collection, which are designated for the temporal and sanctoral cycles of the liturgical year and for the common feasts, the *De diversis* sermons were composed for specific occasions not scheduled on the liturgical calendar. They are, therefore, not tied to specific Scriptural readings assigned in the lectionary, and Innocent's choice of Biblical texts and topics for each sermon can be seen as significant.

Also translated here is the introductory letter sent by Innocent to Arnald, the abbot of Cîteaux, together with a collection of sermons.[55] This letter customarily appears as a "Prologue" in the manuscript collections, even those that are incomplete.[56] It is appropriate that the letter be included here not only for this reason, but also because it outlines Innocent's concept of the nature and importance of preaching.

The Migne collection is taken from the 1575 Cologne edition of the sermons, which is a somewhat faithful repetition of the first edition of 1552.[57] Migne also includes a sermon entitled "Ad Claustrales" (Sermon Five) which was written by Alan of Lille.[58] It may have been incorporated into the Innocent collection as an ex-

ample of what a good sermon should be; and because the theme is
unity among the clergy, it may be a reinforcement of Innocent's
overall vision of clerical reform, a principal topic in these sermons.
We have not translated this sermon. In addition to those printed
in PL, the edition of Sermon Three by Connie Mae Munk has
been helpful.[59] Finally, we have consulted *British Library Additional
18,331 (BL Add.)*, a thirteenth-century manuscript of Innocent's sermons with an excellent text, for the Letter to Arnald (Prologue)
and for Sermons One, Two, Three, Four, and Seven.[60] Only for
Sermon Six have we relied on PL alone, and there we found no
egregious problems.

We have retained Migne's ordering of the sermons, but have
adapted the following titles after considering other available
sources:

> One, In Council of Priests;
> Two, On the Consecration of the Supreme Pontiff;
> Three, On the First Anniversary;
> Four, On the Consecration of Pontiffs;
> Six, Convening the Fourth General Council of the Lateran;
> Seven, In Synod.[61]

The PL ordering of the sermons *De diversis* cannot be accepted
as chronological. Sermon Two was for Innocent's consecration,
February 22, 1198; Sermon Six opened the Fourth Lateran Council,
November 11, 1215.[62] These dates are certain. It seems likely that
Sermon Three was preached for a commemoration of the first anniversary of the consecration, because in it Innocent refers to the
listeners' celebrating the anniversary "today first with me." He further notes that the anniversary commemoration was postponed in
deference to the Feast of St. Peter's Chair at Antioch, which occurs
on the same date. Sermon Four may also have been an anniversary
sermon because it includes a discussion of papal responsibilities.
Giuseppe Scuppa has pointed out that Sermons One and Seven
were synod sermons,[63] which is consistent with *BL Add*. The con-

tinued placement of these two sermons as the first and last sermons of the group is felicitous, because they provide an appropriate introduction and conclusion to Innocent's preaching on the nature of the priesthood. Sermon One focuses on the sins, delinquencies, and responsibilities of the clergy, concerns addressed by the pragmatic reform measures instituted at Lateran Council IV, while Sermon Seven describes the mystical culmination of those clerical reforms, thus providing an appropriate and satisfying closure to Innocent's homiletic work.

As for Scriptural passages, we found that the Latin texts fit into Innocent's Latin sentences much more effortlessly than the received English translations fit into the translated English. For this reason, and because Innocent frequently adapts the Latin to his own purposes or memory, we have made our own translations. We have always consulted the Vulgate Latin, realizing that the Biblical texts used in the papal household were not always the same as the Vulgate. We have also consulted the Douay-Rheims English version, itself a translation of the Vulgate, as well as more modern versions such as *The Anchor Bible* and *The New Jerusalem Bible*.[64] Consistent with Innocent's usage, we use the older Vulgate numberings of the psalms. In all cases we cite chapter and verse from the Vulgate.

The text of the PL edition is sometimes garbled and faulty; we have corrected it by comparison with Innocent's other writings and with *BL Add.* However, most differences between PL and *BL Add.* are merely minor variations, accountable for by different copyists. We use brackets [like this] where we fill in a text that may appear only in truncated form in the original, especially Biblical quotations. We have used parentheses (like this) to insert words or phrases for stylistic clarification in understanding the text. The commentary introducing each sermon provides context and identifies the principal focus of the sermon's message. Footnotes, besides citing sources, draw attention to and clarify some of the multifold Scriptural allusions and rich rhetorical overtones that Innocent assumed would be clear for his audience, but which may not be so readily recognizable for modern readers. Now that the *Glossa Ordinaria*[65] is available in a four-volume complete set, we occasionally call attention to the interlinear glosses, which PL does not print; further, this edition's marginal glosses are printed in their fullness, not truncated as in PL.[66] Unless otherwise noted, translations in the notes are ours.

BETWEEN GOD AND MAN

# LETTER TO ARNALD

This letter from Innocent III to the Abbot of Cîteaux was sent to that monastery with a collection of the Pope's sermons at the request of his chaplain Nicholas, a Cistercian monk. The letter is always included as a Prologue to Innocent's sermon collections,[1] and is an important papal document in its own right. It is the first instruction on preaching known to have been written by a pope since the *Pastoral Care* of Gregory the Great, six centuries before. Included here, as Prologue to the *De diversis* sermons, its practical homiletical advice intensifies the meta-pastoral tone of the sermons themselves, which are addressed primarily to the clergy.

The letter is an example of *ars dictaminis*, the art of letter writing, a distinctive literary genre of medieval times.[2] These artistic letters were not informal, personal messages, but rather documents which were in many cases contracts between correspondents. Letters from people in power, such as kings and bishops, were often proclamations, and in some cases they held the force of law. For that reason they were written with great precision of language, and according to highly developed formulas. The expertise required for composing these letters was truly an art for which scholars were strictly trained. Innocent's *Register* collections are examples of the power and importance of these official letters. That the letter to Arnald is an example of this genre is clear from the salutation, a defining feature of *dictaminis*, i.e., the establishment of the respective ranks of the correspondents. The formality of the greeting, despite Innocent's friendship with Arnald and Nicholas, establishes the letter not as a private note, but as an official introduction to the sermons being sent. It is probable, therefore, that the letter was read aloud to all the monks, and was preserved by Arnald as an important papal document.

As a guide for preachers the letter is an admirably concise summary of both the classical and the Christian oratorical traditions. It stresses the importance of strong arguments in presenting a message, and acknowledges the power of emotional appeals. It recommends the adaptation of the message to individual audiences, and praises the beauty of a graceful rhetorical style for rendering the message more attractive. Particular emphasis is placed on the importance of the preacher's credibility. As his model Innocent points to Christ himself as he who set out "to do and to teach." The "doing" is the living of a virtuous life, which must precede the teaching, lest the preacher be seen as a hypocrite, this point being a principal theme of Innocent's own preaching.

Though the letter is timeless in its content, contemporary events add urgency to its message. In 1199, facing a threat to Catholic orthodoxy from heretical preachers, Innocent had written *Cum ex injuncto*,[3] a decretal from which he draws heavily in this letter. His concern was that heretics seemed eager to preach their errors, while the orthodox clergy was often negligent and unprepared for their preaching duties. In *Cum ex injuncto* he warned concerning the apostolic authority to preach that "No one should usurp the office of preaching," and cites Rom. 10:15, "How shall they preach unless they are sent?" as evidence that preachers must be specifically commissioned for their task.[4] He drew on Mt.10:27 to emphasize preaching as a public action, not to be done by unlicensed preachers, especially those who speak in secret assemblies: "'What I say to you in darkness, say in the light, and what you hear with your ears, preach from the roof-tops." This letter transforms the principles expounded in the decretal into a precise and dynamic prescription for putting those principles into action.

Of particular interest in this letter is the introduction of a theme that will recur in the sermons: the significance of the vestments worn by the high priest of Israel, which prefigure elements of the Christian priesthood. Specifically mentioned here are the bells that hung from the hem of the high priest's robe, making their ringing sound as he entered the sanctuary of the Temple. As Jacob Milgrom points out,[5] the biblical details imply a danger zone between the realm of the profane and the realm of the sacred which cannot be traversed carelessly without inviting peril. The priest faces the jeopardy of being unworthy before the Divine and of failing as messenger to and from the Divine. We can see this zone as the "middle ground" or "median" the priest must occupy as one who is to enter the sanctuary and then return to the people. His safety is guaranteed by the sound he makes. For Christian exegetes, the "sound" of the bells can be understood as the voice of the preacher whose virtuous life establishes his credentials as rightful intermediary between God and the people.[6] This concept, of priest as *in medio*, introduced in this letter, is pervasive in Innocent's sermons.

The exact dating of the letter is difficult. During Innocent's pontificate there were two abbots named Arnald, or Arnaud, at Cîteaux, the mother-house of the Cistercian Order, and it is uncertain to which of the two this letter was addressed. Arnald I, called Arnald Amalric, held office from 1201 to 1211/12; Arnald II was elected in 1212 and died in 1217. John C. Moore argues that the sermon collection was sent between 1201 and 1205, making Arnald I the recipient.[7] An early date would coincide with the preaching crusade to convert the Albigensians, which was led by the Cistercians.[8] Stephen J. T. Van Dijk and Joan Hazelden Walker have found references to the monk Nicholas in Cistercian statutes of 1204 and 1205, but give strong evidence that the sermons were sent late in Innocent's pontificate, during the tenure of the second Arnald, sometime between 1213 and 1216.[9]

Innocent ends his letter by deploring the time he must give to the burdens of office, especially the demands of administrative affairs. Part of this disclaimer may be attributed to the *dictaminis* formula for ending letters with pro forma expressions of humility. Yet the intensity of his complaint gives sincerity to Innocent's plea for the prayers of the abbot and his monks.

## LETTER TO ARNALD

Innocent, bishop, servant of the servants of God, to his beloved son Arnald, abbot of the Cistercian Order, greeting and apostolic benediction.[10]

The weighty testimony of the prophet (Isaiah) teaches us: "Blessed are those who sow upon the waters,"[11] for "The seed is the word of God"[12] and the "Many waters" are many peoples.[13] On the contrary, "cursed among the people is the one who hides the seed grain" and he who buries his talent in the ground.[14] For the innkeeper who received two denarii from the Samaritan should pay out more [than he was given];[15] and the servant entrusted by his lord with two talents should gain more profit.[16] For this reason golden bells hung from the high priest's blue tunic, for fear that, going into the sanctuary without a sound, he would die.[17]

Among the many ministries that belong to the pastoral office, the virtue of holy preaching is the most excellent, as (Paul) the preeminent preacher informs us. "The Lord sent me," he said, "not to baptize, but to preach."[18] "Preach the word; be urgent in season, out of season: and in this way do the work of an evangelist."[19] So it is said, "How beautiful upon the mountains are the feet of those who bring good news!"[20] "Cry out, cease not, raise your voice like a trumpet!"[21] The Lord assigned this duty principally to the apostles, saying, "What I say to you in the darkness, speak out in the light, and what you hear whispered in your ear, preach on the rooftops."[22] "Going into the whole world preach the Gospel to all creatures."[23] Indeed preaching has such great power that it calls the soul back from error to truth, and from vices to virtues. It straightens the crooked, and makes the rough road smooth.[24] It confirms faith, increases hope, and strengthens charity. It uproots the hurtful, plants the helpful, and nourishes virtue. It is the road of life, the ladder of salvation, the gate of paradise.

The preacher, then, must have as his own gold, silver, and balsam:[25] in other words, wisdom, eloquence, and virtue, so that he will understand what he is saying, and what he has said and under-stood, he himself will do.[26] For "He who both does and teaches, will be called great in the kingdom of heaven."[27] Otherwise it will be said to him, "Physician, heal yourself,"[28] for he will be like the cursed[29] fig tree that produces leaves without fruit.[30] So, "Every scribe instructed in the kingdom of heaven brings forth out of his own treasure new things and old,"[31] whether he produces as many proofs from the New as from the Old Testament, whether he offers a sermon as much about the freshness of grace as about the antiquity of guilt, whether he preaches as often about the rewards due to those who are new in their goodness, as about the punishments for those "grown old in evil."[32]

Moreover, in speaking of these things, he should speak in different styles according to the different kinds of people and subjects he addresses, as it is said to the bride in the Song of Songs, "We will make you chains of gold, inlaid with silver."[33] "Gold" signifies wisdom, as Solomon attests, "A very desirable treasure rests in the mouth of the wise one."[34] "Silver," on the other hand, signifies eloquence, as the Psalmist says, "The eloquence of the Lord, chaste eloquence, silver tested by fire."[35] It is fitting that the flowers of wisdom are designated by the "golden chains" adorning the neck and the breast of the church, which are her preachers and teachers.[36] They are "inlaid," that is, made distinct and variegated with "silver," that is, eloquence, so that the style of the sermon may vary, depending on the diversity of the subject matter and of the audience. The Apostle (Paul) said, "Wisdom we speak among the perfect;[37] however, among you I judged myself to know nothing except Jesus Christ, and him crucified." And again, "I could not speak to you as to spiritual men, but as to carnal. So I gave you, as to little ones in Christ, milk to drink, not food."[38] Christ, the Uncreated Truth, also said to the wise and perfect, "To you it is given to know the mysteries of the kingdom of God."[39] Whereas to the ignorant and weak he said, "I have many things yet to say to you: but you cannot bear them now."[40] And then he prudently cau-

tioned them, "Do not give holy things to dogs; nor cast pearls before swine,"[41] but be like clean animals, that chew the cud and have
split hooves.[42]

The preacher, then, should have in his possession wine and oil,
rod and manna, fire and water, each to be brought forth aptly in its
proper place.[43] Principally, however, the preacher should aim at
teaching the faith, at forming lives as the foundation of a building
is formed;[44] confirming what he says by authorities, reasons, and
examples, because "A threefold cord can be unfastened only with
difficulty."[45]

Certainly the dust of vainglory often clings to the feet of
preachers. Just as certainly the preacher should shake that dust
from his feet,[46] and wash them in the water of remorse, so that he
is spotlessly clean, "Lest perhaps when he preaches to others, he
himself may become worthless."[47]

Oh, that in this duty of preaching I myself might always have
done what I am saying. Yet I am burdened by the incursions of so
many cases,[48] and entangled by so many complexities of business,
that I inevitably find myself forced to distraction daily, encroached
upon in everything. Truly I am no longer permitted to think, nor
even to breathe. I am so given over to others, in fact, that I seem
absolutely to be stolen from my very self. I fear that, out of solicitude for the temporal matters being heavily pressed upon me by
the ruthless demands of time, I may altogether neglect the care of
spiritual matters, which the duty of apostolic ministry makes more
obligatory for me. Therefore, I have composed and delivered[49]
some sermons to the clergy and to the people—some in literary
language, some in the vernacular[50]—which on the insistence of the
request you made to me through our shared son, brother Nicholas,
my chaplain and your monk, I have faithfully sent to Your Devotion, asking and beseeching in Christ Jesus, that you in return keep
me spiritually commended in your prayers before the most just
judge and most gracious Father.

# IN COUNCIL OF PRIESTS

The opening words of this sermon, addressed to the assembled
clergy of a Roman synod, clearly illustrate Innocent III's concept of
priesthood: the image of the priest as intercessor, interposed between
God and mankind by the power and duties of his office. Then, drawing the parallel between the Aaronide priesthood and that of the
Catholic Church, Innocent applies Levitical norms to the lives and
actions of the clergy. The result is a practical, step-by-step plan to re-
pair the damage done to both the priesthood and to the Christian
community by those clergy who neglect their priestly duties.

The synods at which this sermon and Sermon Seven were
preached were held twice yearly from ancient times. In contrast to the
far fewer ecumenical councils, these synods were aimed specifically at
admonishing the clergy.[1] Indeed, the "synod sermon" could be called
a sub-genre of homiletics because of its specialized nature. That the
synods were customary does not mean that the admonitions were
perfunctory. Innocent knew well enough that the clergy of his time
were generally ill-educated, morally weak, and ripe for corruption
and heresy; that the bishops themselves were often negligent, timor-
ous, and complacent.[2] Innocent had grown up in Rome, a city domi-
nated by high-ranking clergy, and had himself served in the Curia. If
this sermon was delivered after his accession to the papacy, likely
enough some in his audience had also been his electors and even *pa-
pabile* themselves; others he may have made bishops and cardinals,
leaders all.[3] Later at Lateran IV, Innocent will cite God's command
for cleansing the abominations in unfaithful Jerusalem, "In my sanctuary begin!"[4]

The setting for the pericope of the sermon is the ritual blood sacrifice of animals offered to God by the High Priest of Israel in atonement for the priests' sins of omission. The evocation of the sacrificial slaughter makes vivid the seriousness of Innocent's theme. Although any sin is reprehensible in a priest, failure to perform the priestly duties is the greatest sin because it leaves the community helpless in its guilt, bereft of its rightful access to God.[5]

Innocent structures his discourse according to the stages of the divinely mandated ritual of Leviticus 4:3: as the Aaronide priests were to progress from the entrance to the tabernacle of testimony to the altar of sacrifice, so does the penitent proceed through heartfelt repentance and reparation into the divine presence. It is not Innocent's purpose simply to lay blame on the negligent priests. Rather he urges them toward the remedy for their failures: the Sacrament of Reconciliation (Confession, Penance), the means of repentance and reparation for erring clergy, as well as a spiritual corrective to be administered to the laity. Twelfth-century theologians and canonists had discussed the nature and form of Penance, particularly the need for the penitent's contrition of heart, the function and necessity for oral confession, and the question of how often it could and should be repeated.[6] Innocent speaks from a clear and thorough understanding of the sacrament, even including an orderly checklist of points to be considered in making or hearing a good confession.

In setting forth his instruction on the Sacrament of Penance Innocent shows a psychological sensitivity toward his audience that turns the challenge of the sermon's opening text into a true encouragement toward reform. He accomplishes this by first stressing the rational balance needed in prescribing the reparation the penitent is undertake, not too stringent, not too lax. Then he considers the sacrificial death of proud and selfish hearts that is true repentance. Finally, speaking as a priest himself, he appeals to the *esprit de corps* that unites all those who share the unction of Holy Orders, lest the weaknesses of some contaminate the integrity of them all.[7]

## IN COUNCIL OF PRIESTS

*If the priest, who is anointed, sins, making the people guilty, he will offer to the Lord for his sin a young bull without blemish, and he will lead it to the door of the tabernacle of testimony before the Lord, and place his hand on its head, and sacrifice it to the Lord.*[8]

The words that I have spoken to you, dearest brothers, are the words of the Lord speaking to Moses in Leviticus, about atoning for the serious sin of a priest.

Now there are four kinds of persons for whom sacrifices are to be offered; the priest, the prince, the people, and the individual soul.[9] Further, just as the sin of the priest is described first, so it is judged to be the gravest, due both to the dignity of his office and to the perversity of his example. The first is noted when it is said, *If the priest,who is anointed, sins;* the second when it is added, *making the people guilty.* As in Juvenal's satire, "The greater the offender, the more conspicuous is every vice of the heart."[10]

Many actions are trifling for subordinates that are serious for prelates, and many sins are venial for the laity that are mortal sins for the clergy. For "Who will heal the charmer struck by a serpent"?[11] And if a priest sins, who will pray for him? Certainly, the higher the status, the heavier the fall, for to whom more is entrusted, from him more is demanded.[12] "There shall be a severe judgment for those who rule."[13] "To you," priest, "it is given to know the mysteries of the kingdom of God; but to the others in parables."[14] But "The servant who knows the will of his Lord and does not do it shall be beaten with many blows."[15] "To you," priest, "are given the keys to the kingdom of heaven, and whatever you bind upon earth will be bound also in heaven; and whatever you loose on earth will be loosed also in heaven."[16] But woe to you if you kill souls which are not dying or restore life to souls which are not living![17] To you, priest, it is given to consecrate bread and wine into the Body and Blood of Jesus Christ. But, "If you eat unworthily, you eat a judgment for yourself, not discerning the body of the Lord."[18]

How is it that by your sin you make the people guilty? Through you "the name of God is blasphemed among the nations,"[19] for "The son can do only what he sees the father doing,"[20] and he offers in excuse, "It is enough for the disciple if he is like his master."[21] The layman asks, why not commit adultery, when the priest fornicates? Why not commit usury, when the priest is a usurer?[22] Assuredly the priest is worthy of as many deaths as the examples of moral ruin he gives to the people.[23] If the head is infirm the whole body will be feeble, for "the whole head is sick, and the whole heart sad: from the sole of the foot to the top of the head, there is no soundness in it."[24]

When heretics see us sin, they teach that alms should not be given to us, drawing on the authority of Sacred Scripture, which says, "Let the alms sweat in your hands, until you find someone who is just to whom you may give them."[25] It does not say, "until you find a priest who is adulterous, drunken, envious, proud, perjurious, avaricious, committing usury, and such"; but it says, "until you find someone who is just to whom you may give." Offerings, tithes, or first fruits are to be given to ministers of God, not to servants of the devil: for "Whoever commits sin is a slave of sin."[26] When heretics see us sin, they teach that our preaching should not be listened to, proving this by the authority of Sacred Scripture, which says, "God said to the sinner, 'Why do you expound my laws and put my covenant in your mouth?'"[27] When an offensive mediator is sent to intercede, the animosity of the angry plaintiff is provoked to worse things,[28] because, if his life is despised, it follows that his preaching is held in contempt, and it may be said to him, "Physician, heal yourself;"[29] "First cast the beam out of your own eye; and then take the mote from your brother's eye."[30] The prophet also, before he is commissioned to preach, is first cleansed of sin, and his mouth is touched with a coal taken from the altar with tongs.[31] When heretics see us sin, they teach that we cannot confect the church's sacraments, citing the authority of Scripture, which says, "I will curse your blessings,"[32] "and when you increase the number of your prayers, I will not listen to you, for your hands are filled with blood."[33] "Whatever the unclean has touched will be unclean."[34] Therefore, let our light shine before men so that they may see our good works and glorify our Father who is in heaven.[35]

*If* then *the priest, who is anointed, sins, making the people guilty, he will offer to the Lord for his sin a young bull without blemish.* It is not enough for the priest to offer for his sin a turtledove or a pigeon, a kid-goat or a lamb, a female goat or a sheep. He must offer a *young bull;* not of any quality whatsoever, but one *without blemish;* not just anywhere, but *at the door of the tabernacle;* not before anyone he pleases, but *before the Lord;* nor in any manner he pleases, but *he will place his hand on its head, and sacrifice it to the Lord.* For the sinful soul it is commanded that he offer a *female goat;* for the sinful prince it is commanded that he offer a *male goat;* but for the sin of the priest, just as for the sin of the people, it is commanded that a *young bull without blemish* must be offered. From this the conclusion must be drawn that the sin of the priest is equivalent to the sin of the whole people, because the priest, in his sin, brings guilt down upon the people. Therefore, let *the priest offer* for his sin *a young bull without blemish,* because a great sin must be atoned for by a great victim.

*The young bull without blemish* symbolizes the contrite spirit, since "An afflicted spirit is a sacrifice to God, and God does not despise a contrite and humble heart."[36] This *young bull,* this victim, this sacrifice should be offered to the Lord for sin, so that the *young bull* which by sinning had been unrestrained in its pride, might by repentance be restrained through humility, and put on the yoke of Christ, of which he says in the Gospel, "My yoke is sweet and my burden light."[37] "Then God will accept the sacrifice of justice; then you will lay young bulls upon His altar."[38] In this way, *let the priest lead the young bull to the door of the tabernacle* by confessing his sins,[39] and *place his hand on its head* by deeds of atonement, and *sacrifice it to the Lord* by heartfelt contrition, so that sins of thought may be washed away in the heart, sins of speech in the mouth, sins of deed by good actions, so that the young girl is raised from the dead at home, the young man at the gate, Lazarus in the tomb.[40]

In this way, then, let the priest lead the young bull *to the door of the tabernacle*. If we understand the *tabernacle* to be the body in which, according to the Apostle, "we are absent from the Lord,"[41] surely by the *door of the tabernacle* we should understand the mouth of the body, of which David says, "Place, O Lord, a guard at my mouth, a door round about my lips."[42] To this door the young bull is led when the secret of the heart emerges through confessing his sins. "Speak your iniquities," it (Scripture) says, "that you may be acquitted."[43] "For the innocent man is his own first accuser."[44] He who accuses[45] himself before God, God will excuse him, and he who excuses himself before God, God will accuse him. Let us turn to the Gospel where we will find an example: "Two men went up to the temple in order to pray."[46] The confession of a crime in a human court is vastly removed from one made in the divine tribunal, for one condemns, while the other pardons.[47] In the one, the guilty person confesses and is punished; in the other, the guilty person is absolved; and for that reason the Prophet begs God, "Let not the deep swallow me up, nor the mouth of the pit close over me."[48]

Moreover, great care must be taken lest one *lead to the door of the tabernacle* not *a young bull*, but a fox. For anyone who reveals his sins only in part, and partially hides them, or confesses one part of a sin to one confessor and another part to another, or discloses the fact of the sin while suppressing the intention behind it, or minimizes and makes excuses for his offense—that one clearly leads forward not a young bull, but a fox: for, "Foxes have holes, and the birds of the air nests."[49] "May we," however, as the prophet says, "offer the young bulls of our lips,"[50] confessing altogether every circumstance by which we have sinned the more: in place, in time, in number, in person; according to age, according to knowledge, according to the kinds of sin and their sequence; if done easily, frequently, openly, or persistently.[51]

This is commanded: that the young bull be led *to the door of the tabernacle before the Lord,* who "searches desires and hearts."[52] "All things are open and naked to His eyes,"[53] from whom no secret lies hidden, and whom nothing hidden deceives. Indeed, in the human court, when the guilty one confesses a sin, the judge must pass sentence; in the divine court, when the guilty confesses a sin, the Lord forgets it, for at whatever hour the sinner will have converted and been contrite, then the Lord says, "I will forget all his iniquities."[54] So let the priest to whom the sinner confesses, not as to a man, but as to God, beware lest perhaps after the confession is heard he remembers the sin—that is, lest by word or sign he might indicate that he knows the fault—since it is not said that the *young bull* be brought *to the door of the tabernacle* before man, but *before the Lord.* In fact, the priest who reveals the sin sins more gravely than does the man who commits the sin.

The text continues: And let him *place his hand on its head.* By the *head* of the young bull is represented the governance of the mind, the power of reason, as in "Anoint your head and wash your face."[55] The *hand* represents service, as in the text: "My life is continually in my hands."[56] Thus we *place* our *hand on the head of the young bull* when we base our service on reason. As the Apostle says, "Let our service be rational," so that "we may produce fruits appropriate to repentance."[57] The hand has five fingers, as atonement has five parts: roughness in dress, abstinence from food, perseverance in prayer, interruption of sleep, and largess in alms. The Prophet (David) says of these in the psalm, "I put on sackcloth; I humbled my soul with fasting, and I withdrew my prayer into my bosom,"[58] and, "I rose at midnight to praise You."[59]

But in all these things he should place his hand on the *head* of the young bull so that his service may be reasonable, lest perhaps, if the beast is overloaded, it may stumble; but if burdened too little, it may become wanton.[60] The quality of repentance having been weighed, the degree of punishment should then be in proportion to the degree of guilt: it should not be so light that he will be presumptuous, nor so heavy that he will despair. "I speak humanely because of the weakness of your flesh. For as you once surrendered your bodies to iniquity, serving impurity in sinfulness, so now submit them to serve justice in sanctification."[61] Woe to those who "strain out a gnat and swallow a camel," who "bind up heavy and insupportable burdens, and lay them on men's shoulders; but with their own finger will not move them."[62]

So, *let the priest place his hand on the head of the young bull and sacrifice it to the Lord.* To *sacrifice* the young bull is to crush the heart, "so that," according to the Apostle (Peter), "it may die to sin and live to justice."[63] When it is killed in this way, then it is given new life; when it is struck in this way, then it is healed. "I," says the Lord, "will kill and I will give life; I will strike and I will heal."[64] Therefore let our *young bull* be killed—let it be immolated—so that it may not rise up to sin again. "It is the scoffer, not the penitent, who continues to do what he claims to repent."[65] "The dog returned to his vomit"[66] is the penitent once more at his sin. Now there are indeed some who offer the young bull, but do not immolate it: these are those who repent of one sin, but delight in another. It is futile for anyone to repent unless he repents of all, because God does not pardon by halves. He healed the whole man on the Sabbath.[67] He cast out seven demons simultaneously,[68] the number seven showing that all the sins were forgiven. From another he drove out a legion of demons,[69] showing that whatever sins are in a person, it is necessary to repent of them all. If, as the Gospel says, sins that have been forgiven return because of one new sin, then by how much more are all sins retained because of the one unabsolved sin?[70]

*If,* therefore, *the priest, who is anointed, sins making the people guilty, he shall offer to the Lord for his sin a young bull without blemish, and he will lead it to the door of the tabernacle of testimony before the Lord, and place his hand on its head, and sacrifice it to the Lord.* Therefore, dearest brothers, let us live our lives not only blamelessly, but also prudently. Blamelessly, lest we contaminate the unction of Orders, which we have received. That is, *If the priest, who is anointed, sins,* as if to say, "The priest is not to sin, lest he contaminate the unction." Or this reference to the unction is added to exclude those who, although of the priestly family, could not be anointed and were unfit to minister because they were blemished of body.[71] Let us also live prudently lest we corrupt others by our example, according to the words, "making the people guilty," as if to say, "Let him not sin lest by sinning he corrupt the people." Or, according to the Hebrew text, "If the priest who is anointed commits a sin that brings the people to guilt," that is, if he does what would be sinful for the laity, then that action is all the more condemnable in the priest. Let us preserve, therefore, the sanctity of our hearts and bodies as befits ministers of God and priests of God, the Lord Jesus Christ sustaining us, who is over all things, God, blessed forever. Amen.

SERMON TWO

# ON THE CONSECRATION OF
# THE SUPREME PONTIFF

Innocent III composed this sermon for the occasion of his consecration as Bishop of Rome, February 22, 1198, the Feast of St. Peter's
Chair at Antioch, six weeks after his election as Pope.[1] The Gospel
reading for the feast day included the "Tu es Petrus" account of Peter's being chosen by Christ as head of his church, an appropriate
text for a papal sermon. However, the newly consecrated Pope, ignor-
ing the Petrine passage, took as the pericope for his inaugural sermon
the parable of the "faithful and prudent servant," a text from the
consecration ceremony that had just occurred. In that choice he
placed himself in the age-old tradition "servus servorum Dei," the
Pope as "the servant of the servants of God."

By invoking the theme of episcopal and papal servanthood, Innocent followed two great models: Pope Gregory the Great's instruction
for pastors, *Liber Regulae Pastoralis (Pastoral Care)*, and Saint Bernard's
advice to Pope Eugenius III, *De consideratione (Concerning Contemplation)*.
Gregory and Bernard were deeply spiritual men who were also powerful leaders, intensely involved with the distracting and demanding
daily problems of administration, a situation Innocent had already
encountered in the weeks since his election. It was understandable
that the young Pope would turn to these experienced authorities for
guidance in his new role. It is especially Bernard's considerations of
papal ministry that echo frequently throughout this sermon, indicating that Innocent had studied the saintly abbot's admonitions to an
earlier Pope, and had taken them to heart.[2]

Gregory, Bernard, and Innocent all portray the Gospel servant first as a field worker, assigned like Jeremiah to heavy labor: "I have constituted you today over the nations and over kingdoms, to root up and to pull down, and to waste and to destroy, to build and to plant."[3] This is God's commission to the young and reluctant prophet. Bernard is clear: "Learn that you need a hoe, not a scepter, to do the work of the Prophet. Indeed, he did not rise up to reign, but to root out."[4] The Pope, then, was ordered to work in the field of the Lord, "which is uncultivated out of neglect or uprooted by deceit."[5] Bernard left no room for doubt that whatever power the Pope holds, "a ministry has been imposed upon us rather than a dominion bestowed,"[6] a mandate that Innocent reiterates, word for word.

Bernard then stresses the Pope's stewardship, the work of the servant given charge of the household. This servant, though not the lord of the estate, nevertheless "should preside in order to provide, to counsel, to administer, and to serve."[7] Here we find again Innocent's favorite theme of priest and prelate as intermediaries between God and mankind, God's household. Not to be overlooked is the eschatological import of the Gospel servant's position. The contract to which Innocent was bound carried with it, as he notes, the powers necessary for carrying out his commission, and he was not reluctant to claim those powers. However, the time of the master's return would also be the time for the servant's giving an account for his use of those powers. Toward the end of his pontificate, at Lateran Council IV, Innocent would recall this commissioning of his priesthood and consecration, and attest that the master's return will find his servant still faithfully guarding the household.

The structure of this sermon is based on a series of rhetorical questions: *quis, quem, qualem, quid, quare, quando.* Finding the answers to the questions is an efficient mechanical method for content development that is familiar to all writers, and is especially characteristic of scholastic study. The content generated by this method might easily be dismissed as pedestrian and unoriginal. Yet Innocent himself warns against such an evaluation of the material, telling his listeners to, "Weigh every single word." By providing that critical focus he dispels any notion that this is simply a formulaic discourse.

Innocent's choice of text and content for this sermon must be viewed against the magnificent setting in which it was delivered. According to custom, the consecration of the pontiff took place at St. Peter's Church, the tomb of the "Prince of the Apostles." It was preceded by a triumphal procession through the magnificently decorated city streets. It was attended by all the clergy of Rome, including the cardinals, as well as whatever bishops, kings, princes, and other dignitaries could make the journey to Rome to witness the ceremony. The lavishness of the celebration could not have been matched by even imperial standards. Indeed, if there had been an emperor at the time, he would have been the one to lead the papal mount on foot through the cheering throngs.[8] The Bishop of Ostia consecrated the pontiff and invested him with the mitre as a sign of his spiritual jurisdiction and ministerial position. The sermon, according to ancient custom, was delivered immediately after that ceremony, and Innocent's message dealt with those spiritual and ministerial matters alone. It was only afterward, on the steps of St. Peter's, at the moment he mounted his horse to return to the palace of the Lateran, assisted by the senior cardinal-deacon, that he crowned himself with the tiara, the regal headdress symbolizing his secular authority, and with that gesture took up the additional secular and political responsibilities with which his life would henceforth be largely consumed.

## ON THE CONSECRATION OF
## THE SUPREME PONTIFF

*Who, do you think, is the faithful and prudent servant whom the Lord has constituted over his household that he may give them food in season?*[9]

The character of the servant who is constituted over the household, and the way in which he should be constituted over it, is clearly proclaimed by Truth himself.[10] The servant should be *faithful and prudent, to give them food in season: faithful,* to give them food, and also *prudent,* to give it *in season.* Also clearly described is the one who makes the constitution: the *Lord;* and the one he constitutes: a *servant;* the kind of person he constitutes: equally *faithful and prudent;*

over what he constitutes him: *over the household*; why he constitutes him: so that *he may give them food*; when: *in his season*. Now, let us weigh every single word, for when the words are from the Word, nothing in them is weightless, but all are laden with fruitful meaning.

The *Lord*, then, not just any lord, but he who "has inscribed on his vestment and on his thigh, king of kings and lord of lords,"[11] of whom it is written that "Lord is his name,"[12] has through his very self constituted the primacy of the apostolic seat, so that no challenge can oppose its ordinance—just as he has guaranteed, "You are Peter, and upon this rock I will build my church, and the gates of hell shall not prevail against it."[13] In fact, since he is both the founder of the church and its foundation, truly the gates of hell cannot prevail against it, because the foundation perseveres immovable. As the Apostle (Paul) says, "the foundation has been laid; no other can be put in its place, which is, Christ Jesus."[14]

Therefore, although the boat of Peter is often tossed by great waves in the midst of the sea, yet, especially when Jesus sleeps in it, it is never submerged, because Jesus commands the wind and the sea, and a great calm ensues, so that men marvel at it and say, "What kind of man is this, for the winds and the sea obey him?"[15] This is indeed the sublime and unshaken house[16] of which Truth says, "The rain fell, the floods came, the winds blew and beat upon that house and it did not fall, for it was founded on a rock,"[17] clearly on that one rock of which the Apostle says, "The rock was Christ."[18] It is clear, then, that the apostolic seat does not fail in adversity, but even flourishes by God's promise, so that it can say with the Prophet (David), "In adversity, you made me prosper."[19] It moves forward confident in his promise to the apostles, "I will be with you all days, even to the consummation of the world."[20] And, "If God is with us, who can be against us?"[21]

Certainly, since this ordinance is not from man but from God—or rather more truly—since this ordinance is from the God-man, in vain labors the heretic or schismatic, in vain labors the treacherous wolf, who tries to destroy the vineyard, to tear the tunic, to overthrow the candlestick, to extinguish the light.[22] As Gamaliel, the esteemed doctor of the Law, once said, "If this counsel is of men, it will be refuted; if it is truly from God, you will not be able to refute it, or lest perhaps you may be found fighting against God."[23] "The Lord is my helper, I will not fear what man may do to me."[24]

For I am that *servant* whom God constituted over his household, and I pray that I may be *faithful and prudent*, so that I may *give it food in season!* Entirely a servant—even more: "the servant of servants."[25] I pray that I am not one of those of whom Scripture says, "Whoever has committed sin is the slave of sin";[26] of whom it says, "You worthless servant, I forgave you all the debt";[27] and again, "The servant knowing the will of his lord and not doing it, shall be beaten with many blows";[28] but rather one of those to whom the Lord says, "When you have done all things well, say that we are useless servants!"[29]

I acknowledge myself to be a servant and not a lord. As the Lord says to the Apostles, "The kings of the nations lord it over their people, and those who have power among them are called benefactors.[30] However, not so with you! For whoever is greater among you will be the servant of all, and he who leads will be a minister."[31] For that reason I claim for myself a ministry; I do not usurp a dominion,[32] in the example of my first and chief predecessor, who says, "Not as lording it over those allotted to you, but becoming an example for the flock with all your soul,"[33] and also in the example of the one who said, "They are the servants of Christ; as I say less wisely, I am more [of a servant]."[34] It is a great honor that I am constituted over the household; but a great burden that I am the servant of the whole household.[35] "I have a duty to both the wise and the foolish."[36]

There are few who can serve even one person competently, how much less can one person competently serve everyone! "Who is weak, and I am not weak? Who is scandalized and I do not burn?

Besides those problems which are extraneous, my daily anxiety is my solicitude for all the churches."[37] How many anxieties and sorrows, how many cares and labors I sustain, I can more easily bear than I can utter. I do not wish to dwell on what I bear, for fear I may lose the strength to sustain what I carry. "Day pours out to day" how many labors I sustain, and "night makes known to night" my duties.[38] "My strength is not the strength of stone, nor is my flesh brass."[39] Moreover, even though I may fail through weakness, "my capability comes from God,"[40] "who gives to all men abundantly and does not reproach them."[41] For that reason, although "The path of man is not his own,"[42] I hope, nevertheless, that my steps are directed by him who lifted up blessed Peter as he walked on the waves, lest he sink;[43] who "turned the crooked roads into straight, and changed rough ways into smooth."[44]

You have heard the stipulation, now hear the obligation.[45] Because I am a servant, I am obliged to be *faithful*[46] *and prudent, so that I may give the household food in season.*

Above all else, God requires of me the three duties which are noted in these words, namely: "faith" of heart, "prudence" in works, and "food" for the mouth. That is, that I may be faithful in heart, be prudent in my works, and give food for the mouth. "For we believe in our hearts so we can be righteous, and we confess our faith with our mouth so we can be saved."[47] "Abraham believed God and he was judged to be righteous."[48] "Without faith it is impossible to please God,"[49] because "All that is not from faith is sin."[50] In fact, unless I am grounded in faith, how can I make others firm in faith? It is certain that faith belongs especially to my office. The Lord publicly proclaimed it: "I," he said, "have prayed for you, Peter, that your faith may not fail, and you, once being converted, must confirm your brothers."[51] He asked, and he received, because "He was heard in all things by virtue of his reverence."[52] For that reason the faith of the apostolic seat has never failed even during turbulent times, but has remained whole and unharmed, so that the privilege[53] of Peter continues to be unshaken. So necessary is faith for me as Pope, that, while I have God alone as the judge of my other sins, I can be judged by the church only for any sin committed against the Faith. For "he who does not believe, is already judged."[54] I believe—I most certainly believe—what I may believe as a Catholic,[55] confident that my faith is bound to save me just as the promise says, "Your faith has saved you. Go, and sin no more."[56]

But "Faith without works is dead."[57] Only the faith that works through love is alive because "The just man lives by faith."[58] "For those who are just before God are not only hearers of the Law, but doers."[59] "For if someone is a hearer of the word, and not a doer, he will be compared to a man seeing the face he was born with in a mirror."[60] For that reason faith is not sufficient without prudence, nor is prudence sufficient without faith. It is necessary, then, that I be both *faithful* and *prudent*, for it is written, "Be as prudent as serpents."[61] O how vital prudence is to me, so that my service may be reasonable,[62] so that my left hand may not know what my right hand is doing;[63] so that I can discern between what is leprous and what is clean,[64] between good and evil, between light and darkness, between sacred and profane, lest I call evil good, or good evil, lest I think that darkness is light, or light is darkness,[65] lest I kill souls that are not dying, or restore life to souls that are not living.[66]

Of all the vestments of the High Priest, the Logion directly bears on this point, because it was quadrangular and doubled over.[67] Just so the pontiff's understanding, which the Logion presignified in place and in name, must make a fourfold discernment: between true and false, lest he deviate in what is to be believed; between good and evil, lest he deviate in what is to be done. He must also make a twofold discernment: for himself and for the people, lest "If the blind lead the blind, they both fall into the pit."[68] It was quadrangular because of the fourfold understanding of the scriptures that the pontiff must have: historical, allegorical, tropological, and anagogical. And it was doubled over because of the two testaments, which it is detrimental for the pontiff to ignore, because "The letter kills, but the spirit gives life."[69] It was quadrangular by reason of the New Testament, which is contained in four gospels; and doubled by reason of the Old, which is inscribed on two tablets. O how great should be the quintessential prudence which must correspond to every learned authority,[70] solve complex problems, unlock ambiguities, explain the merits of cases, oversee the disposition of judgments, expound the Scriptures, preach to the people, reprove the restless, comfort the weak, confound heretics, strengthen Catholics. "Who is he, and we will praise him?"[71] The Lord expressly addressed this point, *Who do you think is the faithful and prudent servant?* Such should he be who is constituted *over the household.*

I have indeed been constituted *over the household.* In as much as the most eminent position is mine, so also must my service be the most eminent. Truly it adds to the great praise of the powerful Lord, that through a lowly servant he works his gracious purpose, so that nothing may be ascribed to human ability, but everything attributed to divine power. Yet who am I, or what is my father's house,[72] that I may be seated more eminently than kings, and may occupy the throne of glory? For to me it is said in the Prophet (Jeremiah), "I have constituted you over nations and kingdoms, that you may root up and destroy, lay waste and scatter, and that you may build and plant."[73] To me also it is said as to the Apostle (Peter), "To you I will give the keys to the kingdom of heaven, and whatever you bind on earth, will be bound also in heaven; and whatever you loose on earth, will be loosed also in heaven."[74] When he spoke to all the apostles, he said in particular, "Whose sins you forgive, they are forgiven them, and whose sins you retain, they are retained."[75] When, on the other hand, he spoke to Peter alone, he said universally, "Whatever you bind on earth will be bound also in heaven; and whatever you loose on earth, will be loosed also in heaven,"[76] because Peter can bind the others, but he cannot be bound by others. "You," he said, "will be called Cephas,"[77] which is translated "head," because the fullness of all the senses exists as in the head, while in the other members there is only a part of the fullness.[78] This is the way the others are called to a share of the responsibility, yet Peter alone has received the fullness of power.

Here now you see who that servant is who has been constituted over the household: clearly the vicar of Jesus Christ, successor of Peter, anointed of the Lord, the god of Pharaoh;[79] constituted mediator between God and mankind; on this side of God, but beyond man; less than God, but greater than man; who judges all cases but is judged by no one, declaring in the voice of the Apostle (Paul), "He who judges me is the Lord."[80] Nevertheless, let the office of servant humble him, whom it exalts to the summit of sublimity, so that the sublimity may be humble and the humility may be sublime, for "God resists the proud, but he gives grace to the humble."[81] "He who humbles himself shall be exalted, and he who exalts himself shall be humbled."[82] "Every valley shall be filled, and every mountain and hill be made low."[83] Wholesome counsel: "The greater you are, humble yourself in all things!"[84] Also, "They have made you their leader. Be not exalted; be among them as one of them."[85] This is the light placed on the candlestick,[86] that the sheep who are in the house may see. Further, "if this light is darkened, how much greater shall the darkness itself be!"[87] This is the salt of the earth. "But if the salt loses its savor, how shall the earth be salted? It is good for nothing anymore but to be thrown out, and be trodden on by men."[88] So "To whom more is entrusted, more is demanded [of him]."[89] In fact, he has more reason to fear [for himself], than to glory in, having to render an account to God, not only for himself, but for all who are committed to his care.

Moreover, absolutely all who are of the Lord's household have been placed under his care. Clearly the Lord does not distinguish between this or that household, nor is it said in the plural, over "households," as if there are many; but it is said in the singular, *over the household*, as only the one, so that "There shall be one fold and one shepherd."[90] "One," he says, "is my dove, my perfect one,"[91] and one also is the seamless tunic undivided.[92] There was only one ark, and those within it, gathered under one leader, were saved in the cataclysm; those left outside it, all perished in the flood.[93]

For this purpose, indeed, is he constituted *over the household: that he may give them food in season.* The Lord Jesus Christ constituted the primacy of Peter, before the passion, during the passion, and after the passion: before the passion when he said, "You are Peter, and upon this rock I will build my church . . . and whatever you shall bind on earth, will be bound also in heaven, and whatever you loose over the earth will be loosed also in heaven;"[94] during the passion when he said, "Simon, Satan has desired you that he may sift you like wheat, but I have prayed for you, that your faith may not fail, and you, once converted, confirm your brothers;"[95] and after the passion when he commanded three times, "If you love me, feed my sheep."[96] In the first is expressed the sublimity of the power, in the second the constancy of the faith, in the third the pasturing of the flock. These duties are very clearly shown in regard to Peter in our text: constancy of faith when it is said, *He is constituted over the household;* pasturing the flock when it is said, *that he may give them food.*[97] He is duty-bound *to give* the *food* of example, word, and sacrament— as if he is saying, "Feed them by the example of your life, by the word of your teaching, by the sacrament of the Eucharist—by the example of your action, by the word of your preaching, by the sacrament of Communion." Truth says of the first, "My food is to do the will of him who sent me."[98] Scripture says of the second, "She fed him with the bread of life and understanding, and gave him the water of wholesome wisdom to drink."[99] The Lord says of the third, "My flesh is food indeed, and my blood is drink indeed."[100]

I am duty-bound to *give the food* of example to the household so that my light may shine before men, and those seeing my good works may glorify the Father who is in heaven.[101] "For no one lights a candle and puts it under a basket, but on a candlestick, so that it may shine on all who are in the house."[102] As the Lord says elsewhere, "Let your loins be girt, and lamps burning in your hands."[103] Let one curtain draw another, and let whoever hears this say, "If the priest, who is anointed, sins, he makes the people guilty,"[104] for "The greater the offender, the more conspicuous is every vice of his heart."[105]

But I am also duty-bound to *give the food* of the word to the household, so that by distributing the talent I have received I may multiply it,[106] so that I may accomplish the work of an Evangelist. For, according to the word of the Apostle (Paul), "God did not send me to baptize, but to evangelize,"[107] so that "the whelps may eat the crumbs fallen from their masters' tables,"[108] because "not by bread alone does man live, but by every word that proceeds from the mouth of God."[109] Lest perhaps because of me—or rather more truly against me—it can be said, "The little ones begged for bread, and there was no one who would break it for them."[110]

I am also duty-bound to *give the food* of the Sacrament to the household, so that they may receive life in it and escape death—as he himself says, "I am the living bread which came down from heaven. If anyone eats this bread, he shall live forever. And the bread that I will give is my flesh, for the life of the world. For unless you eat the flesh of the Son of Man and drink his blood, you shall not have life in you."[111]

I am duty-bound to give this threefold food, but *in season*, since according to the proverb of Solomon, "Every good thing in its season."[112] First I must give the food of example, then the food of the word, so that I may give the food of the sacrament worthily, because "Jesus began to do and to teach,"[113] "leaving us an example that we may follow his footsteps. He did not commit sin, nor was deceit found in his mouth."[114] For, "He who does and teaches, shall be called great in the kingdom of heaven."[115] For that reason, pomegranates hung with golden bells from the tunic of the High Priest [lest entering without them, he die].[116] For, if I teach and do not act, it may rightly be said to me, "Physician, heal yourself,"[117] and, "Hypocrite, first cast the beam out of your own eye, and then you may remove the mote from your brother's eye;"[118] "You who preach against stealing, do you steal? You who preach against committing adultery, do you commit adultery?"[119] God said to the sinner, "Why do you expound my laws, and usurp my covenant by your words?"[120] Certainly if one's life is despised, it follows that his preaching is held in contempt. "I became all things to all men," says the Apostle, "that I might win everyone."[121] "Rejoice with those who rejoice; weep with those who weep,"[122] "so that our service might be rational."[123] "Wisdom we speak among the perfect;[124] among you, however, I judged myself to know nothing except Jesus Christ, and him crucified."[125] Thus I gave you milk to drink, as little ones in Christ, not food,[126] for solid food is for the perfect."[127] Consequently let a man prove himself, and so let him eat of that bread, and drink of that cup, since "He who eats unworthily, eats judgment to himself, not discerning the body of the Lord."[128]

Behold, brothers and sons, I have placed before you the food of the word from the table of Sacred Scripture for you to eat, expecting from you this recompense, asking this exchange in return, that you raise pure hands to the Lord without contention,[129] and that, having faith in your prayer, you ask Jesus Christ our Lord, who is over all things God, blessed forever, to make me worthy to fulfill this duty of apostolic servanthood, which is insupportable by my weak shoulders, to the glory of his name, for the salvation of my soul, for the strengthening of the universal church, and for the benefit of all Christian people. Amen.

# ON THE FIRST ANNIVERSARY

Behind the altar, in the apse of the old Basilica of St. Peter was a mosaic portraying Innocent III as the bridegroom of the Roman church. This stylized picture placed that marriage at the center of salvation history. In the forefront of the picture is Christ, the Lamb of God as described in Revelation 5:9. On one side of Christ, Innocent III, barefoot and wearing a crown, stands facing his bride, the church, who is portrayed as a beautiful woman. At the edges of the picture are the two cities, Bethlehem and Jerusalem, scenes of Christ's birth, death, and resurrection. Above these the figures of St. Peter and St. Paul preside, while the four rivers of Paradise pour down around the Lamb. Over all is the hand of God the Father, while in a corner Adam and Eve symbolize death coming into the world.[1] This representation illustrates the message of Innocent's sermon for the first anniversary of his coronation.

From the very early days of his pontificate Innocent III had faced a thorny administrative and constitutional problem: the controversy surrounding the transferral of bishops from one diocese to another. Serious at any time, this issue could not but be exacerbated in the climate of reform being produced by the policies of Innocent's pontificate. Almost contemporaneously with this sermon Innocent issued on January 21, 1199, the decretal *Inter corporalia*, which dealt with this issue. There he addressed the problem by discussing in terms of "spiritual marriage" the indissoluble bonds he believed to exist between bishops and their dioceses.[2]

The decretal is a well reasoned legal argument, concisely laying out in chancery style the premises upon which the Pope, as the judge of major cases, is making a ruling in a specific situation. When he transposes that argument to the sermon genre, Innocent invests the marriage figure with a new energy, calling upon each bishop and *electus* to understand his union with a diocese not only as a canonical procedure, but also as a bond built upon the more radical structure of loyalty, watchfulness, loving support, and indissolubility, that is, on the structure of the ideal marital bond. It follows for Innocent that any violation of that indissoluble bond was as serious and to be as rarely permitted as any violation of the bonds of matrimony. If bishops are indissolubly united with their sees as husbands are with their wives, then just as the marriage bonds can be dissolved only by God, so the bishops' bonds with their sees can, in Innocent's view, be dissolved only by God's Vicar, the Pope. Pennington has pointed out that "juristically Innocent involved himself in a morass of contradictions" by this explanation, yet he and Imkamp have nonetheless shown that it is central to Innocent's ecclesiology.[3]

As Innocent prepares his argument within the sermon, he refers to his treatise on marriage, *De quadripartita specie nuptiarum*.[4] There he had described four kinds of nuptials: between husband and wife, between Christ and the church, between the individual soul and God, and between God and mankind in the Incarnation. *De quad.* follows each marriage from the initial betrothal of human spouses through to the wedding banquet, where is sung the "Wedding Song in Praise of the *Sponsus* and *Sponsa*," Psalm 44, which Innocent explicates as especially praising the nuptials of the church of Christ. It is a fifth kind of "marriage," that of a church with its bishop, including, of course, that of the Church of Rome and its bishop, the Pope, that is the central topic of this sermon.

The figure of a spiritual marriage between a church and its bishop had already held a certain validity for almost a thousand years. As early as the time of St. Cyprian (d. 258) there existed a tradition that churches allegorically "married" their bishops, so that once consecrated for a see, a bishop was to remain there for the rest of his life.[5] One benefit of this custom was that bishops could not be expelled from their sees or transferred without their consent. Practicality would sometimes override this ideal, of course, and bishops did in fact transfer, but such a practice was problematic.

As Innocent uses the term, "marriage" is a metaphor of relationships, focusing first on the bride who is choosing her groom, and then on the groom, the one who says "yes" to her choice. This mutuality produces the "election" of the bishop. Specifically, a church chose its bishop; the *electus* consented to the choice; and the agreement was confirmed by the archbishop or other competent authority. As in marriage, at each stage of this canonical process the partners acquired rights and duties. Therefore, both practically and canonically, perhaps even theologically, a bishop was not free to move at will from one elected position to another, lest the structural integrity of the church be in doubt as to who was bishop or bishop-elect. Moreover, the "marriage" produced comparable "goods," or benefits resulting from the intimacies of the relationship: fidelity (monogamy), progeny, sacrament (indissolubility).[6] The Bishop of Rome is, of course, unique in that there is no higher authority to confirm the election of the Pope; thus the papal *accepto*, "I accept," spoken in acknowledgment of the electors' choice, made that election binding.[7] "Through his election, therefore, the Roman pontiff-elect instantly acquires full jurisdictional powers and the exercise of those powers, both *potestas* (authority) and *executio* (administration)."[8] Innocent cites the Election Decree of 1059 confirming that the Pope was to administer the church even before his consecration and coronation, especially if conditions in Rome were unsettled, as they often were.[9] He makes it clear that the mutual agreement between the cardinal-electors and himself on his election day was indeed the moment of his marriage to the church. What this establishes is the authority any pope must have, from the moment of his election, over the translation (transferral) of bishops.

The rhetorical form Innocent chose for the presentation of his case is an unusual and ingeniously contrived quasi-legal argument. In it he advances, bit-by-bit, the evidence that proves the identity of the church's bridegroom, rather like an attorney providing material to establish the identity of the participant in a legal action. Innocent neither explains the pericope verse-by-verse nor divides it into topics for analysis. Instead he repeatedly delivers the assertion, "He who has the bride is the bridegroom." Each repetition brings with it a requisite of the bridegroom that obviously applies to Innocent. First, the

groom (Christ) has made Peter/ Innocent "head" of his church.
This is an office held by the husband over his wife. Next, promising
to be doctrinally chaste, thus "faithful," to fulfill his office "indissolubly," and to be spiritually "fruitful," he shares the "goods" of marriage with the bride. Moreover, the bride/ church has pledged reverence for him, and he has promised to care for her. This is the
contract by which a man accepts the bride who has chosen him, thus
coming into possession of her, and thereby becoming her groom. Finally, the bride has given Innocent a dowry, the concrete sign of her
espousals. At each step the conclusion is obvious and inevitable, "He
who has the bride is the bridegroom," no one other than Innocent
himself. The case appears to him to be airtight. Yet, beneath the legal
maneuvering of the argument, there can also be felt the true empathy
so many medieval religious writers had for human love and desire, especially as it unfolds in exegesis.[10] Given Innocent's stunning compre-
hension of Scriptural resonance, it is not difficult to hear him evok-
ing the affectionate ardor of human spouses, a true love which
Innocent believed should bind the bishop to his see, the Pope to the
church.

It is not for himself alone that Innocent makes this case, but for
his successors. In the sermon he makes much of the fact that, as
Pope, he had been chosen from among the bridegroom's friends, that
is, from among his brothers in the clergy of Rome. Moreover the detailed section on establishing who are the "kin" to be included or excluded from contracting marriage is a reassuring guarantee that the
rights of the clerical "family" will be honored. The example he offers
is his own status among the clergy he is addressing. He was chosen
from among the cardinals of Rome, the "friends of the bridegroom."
Any one of them might have been in his place, and any one of them
may yet succeed him. The "voice" of the Christ the Bridegroom has
called him to "go up higher," but the commission he "rejoices" to
hear is that of strengthening his brethren, even while he relies upon
their brotherly comradeship for his own moral support.

Innocent's argument for the Pope's rights is well-crafted and
rhetorically elegant. However, despite his effort, the questions
surrounding the issue of the translation of bishops were not to be finally resolved until the time of Urban V (1363).[11] For Innocent him-

self, however, the case was closed. He and the popes who followed him were to be joined to the church by marriage bonds that were indissoluble. The memorial of the nuptial was the mosaic in Peter's own basilica where the inscription beneath the picture proclaimed:

> This is the supreme See of Peter, the beautiful and splendid Mother of all the churches, which is the sacred temple of the High Priest. May the one designated by Christ, whom he serves in this very temple, receive the flowers of virtues and the fruits of salvation.[12]

## ON THE FIRST ANNIVERSARY

*He who has the bride is the bridegroom; but the friend of the bridegroom, who stands and hears him, rejoices with joy because of the bridegroom's voice.*[13]

It is the groomsman who says these words about the bridegroom; the voice speaks of the Word; the lamp, of the Sun; John, of Christ.[14] For the bridegroom is Christ, and the bride he has is the church.[15] David said of him, "He pitched his tent in the sun, [and like a bridegroom coming out of his bridal chamber, he exults like a giant to run his race]."[16] Solomon says to the bride, "You have wounded my heart, my sister, my spouse."[17]

Indeed we recall that we defined the four types of nuptials in the little book we published on the fourfold figure of marriage.[18] First, between a husband and his lawful wife; second, between Christ and holy church; third, between God and the just soul; fourth, between the Word and human nature. Of the first type of nuptials the first man, waking, prophesied, "Therefore a man shall leave his father and mother, [and cling to his wife and they shall be two in one flesh]."[19] Of the second nuptials John speaks in the Apocalypse, "Come, I will show you the new bride, the spouse of the Lamb."[20] Of the third nuptials the Lord speaks through the Prophet, "I will espouse you to me in justice and judgment, in mercy and compassion."[21] Of the fourth nuptials the bride says in the Song of Songs, "Go out, daughters of Jerusalem, and see King

Solomon in the diadem [with which his mother crowned him in the day of his heart's joy]."[22]

In this fourfold configuration of marriages something can be found that is very worthy of both admiration and veneration. Through the first it comes to pass that there are two persons in one flesh; through the second it comes to pass that there are two in one body; through the third it comes to pass that there are two in one spirit; and through the fourth it comes to pass that there are two in one Person. Of the first, Scripture declares, "They will be two in one flesh."[23] For that reason Truth (himself) added, "Therefore they are no longer two, but one flesh."[24] Of the second the Apostle (Paul) says, "All the members of the body, although they are many, yet are one body in Christ,"[25] and in regard to this same union he adds elsewhere, "Truly we are all baptized into one body."[26] Of the third, Scripture clearly says, "Whoever clings to God is one spirit with him."[27] Of that union John the Apostle says, "Whoever abides in love abides in God, and God in him."[28] Of the fourth, the Catholic faith firmly avows that "As the rational spirit and the flesh is one human being, one Christ is God and man."[29] Of that ineffable union the Evangelist attests, "The Word was made flesh, and lived among us."[30] The first union, then, is carnal, the second sacramental,[31] the third spiritual, and the fourth personal: carnal, as we have said, between a husband and his lawful wife, sacramental between Christ and holy church, spiritual between God and the just soul, personal between the Word and human nature.

Therefore, *he who has the bride is the bridegroom.*

*But the bridegroom's friend stands, and rejoices with joy because of the bridegroom's voice.* I have become that friend of the bridegroom to whom the bridegroom said lovingly, "Friend, go up higher."[32] I have been made the successor of him who in his triple response to the bridegroom said, "Lord, You know that I love You."[33] Would that I might love the bridegroom just as I am loved by the bridegroom! For what more could he do for me to love me more? Certainly he has heaped up the good things[34] of nature in me; he has multiplied in me the gifts of grace; he has brought me spiritual blessings; he has added temporal ones over and above, and I hope that he will grant me eternal ones. "If I were to boast, it would certainly not be advantageous for me,"[35] because "The one to whom more is entrusted will have more demanded from him," according to the law of Truth [himself].[36]

And so *standing*, I rejoice because of his voice—but for which "voice?" Is it the one by which he said to me in Peter, "I will give you the keys to the kingdom of heaven, and whatever you bind on earth will be bound also in heaven"?[37] Or is it that by which he said to me through the Prophet, "I have constituted you over nations, so that you may tear out and destroy, and build and plant"?[38] But because of this "voice" there is more for me to fear in this than to rejoice in. For I know the one who said, "There shall be a severe judgment on those who rule."[39] On the same point Scripture warns and says, "The greater you are, humble yourself in all things."[40] "They have constituted you as the leader. Do not be arrogant; be among them as one of them."[41] And the Lord in the Gospel: "He who is greater among you, let him be the servant of all, and he who is the superior, be the one who serves."[42]

So then, for which "voice" should I rejoice? Certainly for that in which the Lord said to the apostles, "I will be with you all days, even to the consummation of the world,"[43] and specifically to Peter, "Simon, behold, Satan has demanded that he may sift you like wheat: [but I have prayed for you that your faith may not fail: and you, being once converted, confirm your brothers]."[44] This is *the bridegroom's voice* for which I *rejoice:* for just as he who predicts the fight to Simon promises the victory, so he who imposes the duty is he who provides the help. He foretells the fight when he says, "Satan has demanded that he may sift you like wheat." He promises victory when he adds, "But I have prayed for you, so that your faith may not fail." For "This is the victory which overcomes the world, our faith."[45] He imposes the office when he says, "Confirm your brothers." He provides his help when he says, "I have prayed for you, Peter." For "He is heard in all things because of his reverence."[46] "The Lord is my helper, I will not fear what man may do to me."[47]

Therefore, *he who has the bride is the bridegroom.*

But am I not the bridegroom and each of you a friend of the bridegroom? Certainly I am the bridegroom, since I have as my bride[48] the noble, rich, sublime, beautiful, chaste, beloved, sacrosanct Roman church, which is instituted by God to be the mother and teacher[49] of all the faithful. She is Sarah more mature, Rebecca more prudent, Leah more fruitful, Rachel more pleasing, Hanna more devoted, Susanna more chaste, Judith more courageous, Esther more beautiful. "Many daughters have amassed riches; this one alone has surpassed them all."[50] My sacramental union is with her,[51] with her my nuptial consummation. A wondrous thing, that I who promised celibacy have contracted marriage. But this union does not hinder celibacy, nor does the fruitfulness of this union take away the chastity of virginity. John was pleasing in celibacy; Abraham was pleasing in marriage.[52] Would that I may be pleasing in both, so that I may joyfully carry home the harvest[53] of both!

It is customary to say of carnal marriage between a man and a woman that it is initiated, ratified, and consummated: initiated in betrothal, ratified in consent, consummated in intercourse. So also the spiritual marriage, which is between a bishop and his church, is said to be initiated in election, ratified in confirmation, consummated in consecration. However, the marriage which I the bridegroom have contracted with this my spouse was initiated and ratified simultaneously, because the Roman pontiff, "when he is elected, is confirmed, and when confirmed, is elected."[54] Do you not remember what you taught about this in a canon? "Since he is elected, as true Pope he obtains authority for ruling the Roman church and administering all its powers."[55]

Certainly, when I entered the contract, the son led the mother into marriage;[56] when I concluded the contract, the father (pope) had the daughter as wife. In carnal marriage kindred are excluded, and those not of one's blood are admitted; but in "spiritual" marriage, *prima facie*, those not of one's blood are excluded according to the rule, and kindred are admitted. As for excluding kindred from a carnal marriage, you have taught read the prohibition in the canon: "We forbid all kin related by affinity to approach the conjugal bond."[57] As for excluding those not of one's blood from the "spiritual" marriage, however, canonical authority hands it down that: "There is for the clergy the faculty of resisting[58] if they see themselves being imposed upon; and if it happens that someone is brought in against their will, they should not fear to refuse him." To that point a caution is found in the canon that, "Only from among the cardinal priests or deacons may anyone be consecrated to the summit of apostleship."[59]

And so today you celebrate with me the first anniversary day of my consummation of this spiritual marriage. Although I was consecrated in the apostolic seat on the day of blessed Peter the Apostle being constituted to the episcopal chair,[60] just as the light of the sun does not allow the light of a star to be seen, so that greater solemnity does not allow this one to be celebrated at the same time. Therefore, the lesser yields to the greater because the lesser is contingent upon the greater. I contracted the marriage [in election and consent], and I celebrated the nuptials in my consecration.[61]

Principally there are three goods in marriage: fidelity, offspring, and sacrament. Fidelity refers to chastity, offspring to fruitfulness, sacrament to stability.[62] Indeed, such fidelity do the Roman pontiff and the Roman church always safeguard for one another, that the words of Truth [himself] in the Gospel can be fittingly applied to them: "I know my sheep, and mine know me."[63] "They do not follow the stranger, but flee him, since they do not recognize the voice of strangers."[64] "Strangers" are heretics and schismatics, whom the Roman church does not follow, but rather pursues and puts to rout. However, they hear and recognize their own—not the apostate, but the apostolic; not the Cathar, but the Catholic—receiving and returning the conjugal duty; receiving from him the duty of prudent care and returning the duty of reverence. For "a husband has no power over his own body, but his wife does. In the same way the wife has no power over her own body, but her husband does."[65]

Further, since the Roman church may give the duty of reverence to no one other than the Roman pontiff, who has no other superior except God, why is it that the Roman pontiff is obliged to render the duty of prudent care not only to the Roman church in particular, but also universally to all the other churches? "To the wise and to the unwise I have a duty,"[66] the Apostle says, and "My daily urgency is solicitude for all the churches."[67] Perhaps this can be judged comparable to what is written in the Old Testament: that one [husband] may have many [wives], but a wife may have but one husband?[68] Have you not read that Abraham had Sara as his wife, and it was she who brought her maid Hagar to him, but he did not commit adultery by this, but rather fulfilled his duty?[69] So also the Roman pontiff has as his spouse the Roman church, which "brings in to him" the churches subject to her, so that they may receive from him the same duty of care, because the more he has been given, the more he must pay out. Now, however, what was previously done in the flesh, is done in the spirit, since "It is the spirit that gives life; while the flesh can gain nothing."[70]

But cannot one bishopric have two bishops, and one bishop have two bishoprics? We do not need to look very far for examples: one and the same man is Bishop of Ostia and of Velletri, so that each church "wed" him at the same time.[71] Again, the Church of Hippo, which had been "married" to Valerius while he lived, also "wed" blessed Augustine, who did not so much succeed Valerius as accede to him.[72] But you who get such pleasure from disputing questions must ask yourselves how these "marriages" can exist without violating the law of marriage.[73] For myself there is a greater concern that is uppermost in my mind. It is that this union contracted between bishop and church might raise up[74] religious offspring for Christ so that his "wife may be like an abundant vine on the walls of his house; and his children thrive [around his table] like shoots around an olive tree."[75] For the Apostle says, "My little children, with whom I am in labor again until Christ is formed in you."[76] As once Leah, having been given the mandrakes, bribed Jacob to come to her, and she conceived and gave birth.[77] Those, however, whom the church raises up in Christ,[78] she teaches the doctrines of salvation and directs with instruction in virtue: "She feeds them with the bread of life and understanding, and gives them the water of wholesome wisdom to drink."[79] "Come," she says, "eat my bread, and drink my wine, which I have prepared for you,"[80] the heavenly bread and the chalice of salvation, which, "if anyone tastes them, he shall live in eternity."[81] They have in them "everything delicious, sweetness for every taste."[82]

The sacrament between the Roman pontiff and the Roman church perseveres so firm and unshakable that they cannot be separated from one another ever, except by death. The Apostle says that after her husband dies, a wife "is released from the rule of her husband."[83] A husband joined to this wife, does not seek a release, does not leave her, and cannot be dismissed,[84] for "it is according to his Lord that he either stands or falls—and it is the Lord who judges."[85] The Roman church can dismiss the Roman pontiff only because of fornication—I mean not carnal, but spiritual fornication, for the marriage is not carnal but spiritual—and this fornication is the sin of heresy. For "Whoever does not believe is already condemned."[86] In that sentence you can understand what is written in the Gospel you have heard, "You are the salt of the earth, if the salt loses its savor, how shall it be salted?"[87] I, however, can hardly believe that God would permit the Roman pontiff to sin against faith, because he prayed specifically[88] for him in the person of Peter himself. "I," he said, "have prayed for you, Peter, [that your faith may not fail, and you, being once converted, confirm your brothers]."[89]

Therefore, *he who has the bride is the bridegroom.*

This bride, however, did not marry empty-handed, but bestowed on me a dowry, costly beyond price: an abundance of spiritual gifts, and an amplitude of temporal gifts, a magnitude and multitude of both. For while others have been called to a portion of care [for the church], Peter alone has been received into the plenitude of power.[90] As a sign of the spiritual gifts she brought me the miter; as a sign of the temporal she gave me the crown:[91] miter for priesthood, crown for governance, constituting me as Vicar of the one on whose vestment and on whose thigh is written "king of kings and lord of lords,"[92] "a priest forever according to the order of Melchisedech."[93] She gave me a full dowry, but whether I have made her any gift for the nuptials, you may have seen. I do not speak boastfully. She sought out one who was untested; she accepted one who resisted; objecting at first, yet finally consenting, because only consent between persons legally eligible will bring about the marriage.

In this way it can be seen to occur—however strange it may seem—that someone can be pontiff of a church before he is its spouse, just as someone can be spouse of a church before he is its pontiff. For when a bishop, through the provision[94] of a superior is justly given to those wrongfully rejecting him,[95] even before they consent to him, he is truly their pontiff because of the authority of the legal order. But it is probable that he may not yet be their spouse if he lacks their consent, because that church is constrained[96] to give consent if it is to enter the marriage bond with him. Once he is accepted[97] through election, he unquestionably becomes their spouse, because of the mutual consent of the electors and the elect, especially when the election is confirmed. But before he is consecrated, he will claim neither the name nor the office of pontiff.

But our solicitude must question whether this is true. It is possible in spiritual marriages to distinguish between bridegroom and husband, and between bride and wife: the "bridegroom" is called *electus* before confirmation, namely, before he knows her, that is, before he governs her. However, he is called "husband" after confirmation, and most of all after consecration, when he at once fully governs her. Or better said: "bridegroom" or "bride" for virginity, "husband" or "wife"[98] for fruitfulness. "For I have espoused you," says the Apostle, "to one husband, so that I may present you as a chaste virgin to Christ."[99]

Therefore, *He who has the bride is the bridegroom.*

And you, brothers and sons, who are friends of the bridegroom, who rejoice with joy because of the bridegroom's voice, may you lift up "pure hands without contention"[100] to God "from a pure heart, a good conscience, and sincere faith,"[101] begging in prayer, that I so render my conjugal duty to the church, that when the bridegroom comes I may deserve to go in to the nuptial feast with the wise virgins, lamps ablaze,[102] where he himself serves,[103] who is over all things, God, blessed forever. Amen.

# ON THE CONSECRATION
# OF PONTIFFS

In what he himself calls a "terrifying and irrefutable" argument, Innocent III presents the thesis for this sermon in an unusual form, a scholastically framed syllogism. This gives his message an abrupt and exigent introduction, similar in force to the rigorous injunction in the pericope of Sermon One. As that sermon called the clergy to a *metanoia* from laxness to self-sacrifice, so this sermon challenges them to the work for which they were "constituted" at their ordinations, to live out their duty to be the "salt of the earth." The phrase "salt of the earth" has become a commonplace saying today, and has lost much of its power to impress modern readers. However, in Innocent's time, as in its ancient Biblical setting, the metaphor was as powerful in its astringency as salt is in fact[1] and would prove to be a rich source of material for his argument.

For the nomad and early agricultural tribes of Biblical times, salt was a costly and precious necessity for maintaining life in a harsh climate, as it is for desert people even today. Not only did it make their simple and monotonous diet more palatable, but it replenished the natural salt lost in the desert heat, and was therefore a requirement for the health of the people and their herds. It was also essential for the preservation of food, particularly meat and fish, which, if left unsalted, would certainly rot, leaving the people to starve. This ability to prevent decay made salt also a cleansing and healing agent. "Rubbing salt into a wound," was a painful but effective means of preventing infection. In Middle Eastern custom the sharing of salt between and among friends was a pledge of faithfulness and comradeship, a promise of honesty and loyalty. Finally, salt was a part of every ritual sacrifice performed by the priests of Israel, the "covenant of salt" signifying God's enduring promises to the priests themselves.[2] Salt that was too dissolute or too contaminated to perform its other functions was strewn on the roads as a sort of primitive paving, so that its sterilizing function would keep the weeds from growing up along the paths. Three of these functions of salt—the duties of giving savor, preserving goodness, and cleansing evil—are those selected by Innocent for explication here. As "salt," the clergy would perform these duties spiritually.

Once again, as is his practice, Innocent wants to explore with his listeners the meaning of the text for himself, the Pope. He begins this discussion with an analysis of the chemical constitution of salt, a scholastic exercise which by modern standards may appear to be simplistic science.[3] Such an analysis proves fruitful, however, as Innocent unfolds the parallel between the constituents of salt and the constitution of the priesthood, and then extends the parallel to include his own office. Employing one of his favorite models, he judges that whatever is required for those in subordinate positions will be magnified for those in higher places; whatever is constituent for priests and bishops will be more intensely required of the Supreme Pontiff, who is particularly to exemplify "salt." It is the duty of salt to be a contrastive and intermediary agent: to heighten savor for those who feast, to preserve food against hunger, to dry up the wellsprings of rot, decay, and unwanted growth. As the substance salt has the constituent principles of heat and moisture, so are all priests to live lives of charity and wisdom: the "heat" of charity and the "moisture" of wisdom making them effective intermediaries between God and mankind. The Pope, as a man, may be morally sinful, thus lacking the heat of charity, but repentance for such sins can bring forgiveness. However, if the Pope teaches heresy, thereby violating the moisture of wisdom, he betrays his office and must be deposed.[4]

Beneath the scholastic rigor of the sermon's argument lies an emotional warmth that demonstrates a true concern for his brothers in the clergy, and a very real devotion to Christ, whom Innocent describes as "the relish and delight and sweetness of the soul." His own regard for the sermon's importance was shown by his inclusion of it among those to be recited at the papal Matins of the Office of Doctor (teacher) of the Church, a place where its message would be a recurring reminder of the divine commission for the clergy to be, consistently and courageously, the "salt of the earth."

## ON THE CONSECRATION OF PONTIFFS

*You are the salt of the earth. But if the salt loses its savor, in what will it (the earth)*[5] *be salted? It is good for nothing anymore except to be thrown out and trodden on by men.*[6]

In these words set before us, Truth, who cannot be deceived, and who does not want to deceive, introduces a terrifying and irrefutable argument.[7] By setting forth the premise, adding the proposition, and deducing the inference, he designates the office, ascribes the failure, and infers the penalty. He designates the office when he says, *You are the salt of the earth.* He ascribes the failure when he continues, *But if the salt loses its savor, in what else can it (the earth) be salted?* He infers the punishment when he concludes, *It is good for nothing anymore except to be thrown out and trodden on by men.* Therefore, whoever accepts the office must take care lest he incur failure, because he will not evade the punishment.[8] "The mighty shall suffer torments mightily, for the most severe judgment is rendered against those who rule."[9] Certainly, the greater the preeminence, the heavier is the fall, for "The greater the offender, the more conspicuous is every vice of his heart."[10]

So, Christ says, *You are the salt of the earth.*

Among all the virtues and gifts[11] two above all are principally necessary for us: clearly charity and wisdom—charity for the formation of an honest life, and wisdom for the knowledge of true doctrine. For "whoever does and teaches, will be called great in the kingdom of heaven."[12] "For Jesus began to do and to teach,"[13] "leaving us an example, that we should follow in the footsteps of him who did not sin"[14]; so that there would be honesty in our lives

and truth in [our] teaching, "nor was deceit found in his mouth."[15]
It was for that reason that pomegranates with golden bells hung
from the vestment of the High Priest, lest, going up into the sanctuary without them, he would die.[16] For there are many—may I
myself never be in their number—who speak out but do not act.
"They bind up heavy and insupportable burdens and lay them on
men's shoulders, but they are unwilling to move them with a finger
of their own."[17] It can be said to such as these, "Physician, heal
yourself."[18] "You hypocrite, first cast the beam out of your own
eye, and then you may cast out the mote from your brother's eye."[19]
"You who preach against stealing, do you steal? You who preach
against committing adultery, do you commit adultery?"[20]

Clearly these two, charity and wisdom, are praised in [the reference to] salt, which is produced from two things: that is, heat and
moisture, since moisture is condensed by heat to become salt.
Charity is designated by the heat, of which the Lord says, "I have
come to cast fire onto the earth; and what else do I desire except
that it will burn?"[21] "Many waters cannot quench charity."[22] By
moisture, on the other hand, is designated wisdom, of which
Solomon says, "The words from a man's mouth are deep water,
and the fountain of wisdom is an overflowing torrent."[23] The Pontiff, therefore, must be the salt of the earth, so that through charity
he can shape the people by the example of his life, and through
wisdom he can instruct them by the word of his teaching.[24]

Salt principally does three things: it seasons food, dries meat,
renders the ground sterile.[25] What blessed Job says points to the
first: "Can anything insipid be eaten that is not seasoned with
salt?"[26] What is said about the fish in Tobias relates to the second:
"They salted its flesh."[27] What the Psalmist says refers to the third:
"He has turned a fruitful land into a salt marsh, because of the
wickedness of those who live there."[28] This is the kind of salt that
should be in the prelate: to season food, to dry meat, and to render
the earth sterile. He should season the food of teaching, as Truth
says, "Who, do you think, is the faithful and prudent servant,

whom his lord has constituted over his household to give them food in season?"[29]; he should dry the meat of concupiscence, of which the Apostle says, "The flesh lusts against the spirit, and the spirit against the flesh;"[30] and he should render the earth barren of its iniquity, as the Lord says to Adam, "Cursed is the earth in your work. It will bear thorns and thistles for you."[31]

The food of teaching is insipid which is not seasoned by the salt of wisdom, particularly that wisdom of which the Apostle (Paul) says, "Christ is the power of God and the wisdom of God."[32] No teaching tastes good which is not redolent of Christ, who is the relish and delight and sweetness of the soul. Thus the Apostle says, "Let your speech be seasoned with salt."[33] In fact, any discourse is insipid which is not seasoned with the salt of spiritual wisdom. Therefore the sons of the prophets said to Elisha,

> See, the site of this city is very good, but the waters are very bad, and the ground is barren. So he said to them, bring me a new vessel and put salt in it. And he said, 'Thus says the Lord, I have healed these waters, and there shall be no more death nor barrenness in them.'[34]

Elisha, Christ; the city, the Law; the water, the letter of the Law; the salt, wisdom; the vessel, the preacher; the ground, the synagogue. Thus, "The site of this city is very good," because according to the Apostle, "The Law is holy, and the commandment is holy,"[35] "but the water is very bad" because "the letter kills while the spirit gives life."[36] For that reason "the ground is barren"; that is, the synagogue is unfruitful because the Law has led no one to perfection.[37] "The new vessel" is the preacher of the Gospel. Such was the Apostle Paul, of whom the Lord says, "This man will be my chosen vessel [to bring my name before the pagans and pagan kings]."[38] He is called a new vessel because of the new teaching, of which Truth says, "No one puts new wine into old wineskins."[39] "Salt is put into this vessel," as the Lord said to the Apostles, "Have salt in you, and have peace among you."[40] "Out of this new vessel Elisha threw salt into the spring, so he might heal the waters, and there would be 'no more death or barrenness in them.'" Christ, however, through his preachers casts the Gospel into the letter that kills, because "It is the spirit that gives life. The flesh is unable to gain anything."[41] In the same way, at the wedding feast he changed water into wine,[42] and he took the veil from the face of Moses, so that his face being unveiled, he might contemplate the glory of the Lord.[43]

Moreover, the prelate is duty-bound not only to season the foods, but also to dry the meat—to chastise his own body and bring it into subjection, lest perhaps, when he has preached to others, he himself might be worthless.[44] Unless the stream of carnal concupiscence is dried up, the carnal man, like a beast of burden, will surely grow putrid in his own excrement, stinking like a four-day corpse in the tomb.[45] This is why the Psalmist said, "Pierce my flesh with fear of You, for I dread Your judgments."[46] Fear is the best nail, for it fastens our flesh to the cross, as is said, "They have crucified their flesh with its vices and concupiscences,"[47] since "the fear of the Lord drives out sin."[48] It is said of this again through the Prophet, "From our fear of You, O Lord, we have conceived and brought forth the spirit of salvation."[49]

It is also said that victorious kings sowed ruined cities with salt,[50] lest any new shoot might rise up in them again. The "victorious kings" are the holy preachers, of whom the Apostle says, "With their faith the saints conquered kingdoms."[51] The "ruined cities" are the nations converted to the faith, from which the kingdom of the devil is torn down. Of this destruction the Lord speaks through the prophet, "I have constituted you over nations, and over kingdoms, so that you may dig up, and pull down, and devastate, and destroy."[52] Then we must sow these ruined cities with salt, so that whatever is budding in them will not rise up again; so that the thorns and thistles of vice may not sprout from what is left. It is this the Lord enjoins in the Law, "In all your oblations you must offer salt;"[53] that is, add wisdom to all you say or do, lest what you offer to the Lord be foolish or insipid.

*But if the salt loses its savor, in what can it (the earth) be salted?* This insipidness[54] is twofold: one of nature, which is an inconstant condition; the other is a deliberate fault, which is vice and sin. Of the first the Apostle (Paul) says, "The creation is unwillingly subject to weaknesses."[55] "'Vanity of vanities,' says Ecclesiastes . . . 'and all is vanity.'"[56] The Psalmist also says, "All things are vanity, everyone living."[57] Of the second it is said by the same Psalmist, "O you sons of men, how long will your hearts be deadened? Why do you love your weakness and even try to lie about it?"[58] And again, "The sons of men are liars in their self-judgments; they deceive themselves about their own inanity."[59] "As their days dwindled away into triviality, their years were quickly wasted."[60] No one escapes the first [kind of] weakness, just as blessed Job has said, "Man born of woman, living for a short time, is filled with many miseries. He comes forth like a flower, and withers, and slips away as a shadow."[61] But what the Lord says, *If the salt loses its savor, in what else can it (the earth) be salted?* pertains to the second [kind of] weakness. It is as if he had said, "If the prelate becomes dissolute in vice, by whom will the people be instructed?" Now, some lose their savor in the heart, some in the mouth, some in deeds: [those losing it] in the heart are those who believe wrongly; in the mouth, those who teach wrongly; in deeds, those who live wrongly. Of the first the Apostle says, "They grew vapid in their thinking, and their foolish heart was darkened."[62] The Psalmist says of the second, "Everyone of them has spoken inanities to his neighbor. With lying lips and a divided heart they have spoken sinfully."[63] Solomon says of the third, "I have seen all the things that are done under the sun, and, behold, all of it is futile,"[64] because "Admonishing the perverse is hard, and the number of fools is infinite."[65]

Some lose their savor because of moisture, some because of heat, some because of both heat and moisture.[66] Those losing their savor by heat are destroyed by spiritual lusts, such as anger or envy. Of these it is said, "They were inflamed with lust towards her," inflamed from hell.[67] Those losing savor by moisture are destroyed

by carnal lusts, such as gluttony and self-indulgence. Of them it is
said, "Behemoth sleeps in moist places; having trust that the Jor-
dan will flow into his mouth."[68] Those losing their savor because
of both heat and moisture, are ruined by spiritual lusts and carnal
lusts together. Of them—so that the punishment fits the sin—
Scripture says, "They shall pass from the snowy waters to extreme
heat."[69] David says about the first, "Fire has fallen on them, and
they shall not see the sun."[70] About the second Jacob says, "You
are poured out like water; you will not grow great, because you
went up to your father's bed."[71]

So *if the salt loses savor* in the prelate, *by what* will the people *be salted?* As if it says, "By nothing." As divine Law testifies, "If the
priest, who is anointed, sins, making the people guilty."[72] The sin
of the prelate is, therefore, both destructive to others and perilous
to himself: destructive to others because *"If the salt loses its savor, by
what will it (the earth) be salted?"*; perilous to himself because *"It is good
for nothing anymore, except to be thrown out,"* that is, put out of office, and
*"trodden on by men,"* that is, despised by the people. He will be *thrown
out and trodden on by men*, that is, be excommunicated and shunned:
*thrown out* because he has sinned against himself, and *trodden on by
men* because he has sinned against his neighbor.

It is apparent enough how this can be interpreted about other
prelates, but how it should be interpreted about the Roman pontiff
is not yet clear. The servant, according to the Apostle, "By his own
lord stands or falls." Because of that the same Apostle says, "Who
are you who judges another man's servant?"[73] Since the Roman
Pontiff has no other lord than God, then who can throw him out
or trample him underfoot, no matter how much he may lose his savor? When it can be said to him, "Enfold your justification into
your own heart"?[74] Nevertheless he should not mistakenly flatter
himself about his power, nor rashly glory in his eminence or hon-
or, for the less he is judged by man, the more he is judged by God.
I say "less" because he can be judged by men, or rather shown to
be judged, if he clearly loses his savor to heresy,[75] since he "who

does not believe, is already judged."[76] It is only in this case that it should be understood of him that, *If the salt loses its savor, it is good for nothing anymore, except to be thrown out and to be trodden on by men.*

How can one say, *it is good for nothing anymore?* Does the Lord not say, "In whatever hour the sinner will convert and repent, he will live and not die"?[77] Did not the shepherd, leaving ninety-nine sheep in the wilderness, go to seek the hundredth, which was lost, and carry the found sheep back on his shoulders?[78] Did not the woman light a lamp and sweep the house to find the lost drachma?[79] And in each parable, the Lord added that there shall be greater joy among the angels of God over one sinner doing penance than over ninety-nine just men, who do not need to repent.[80] Did David not lose savor when he committed adultery and murder? And yet he was not thrown out nor trampled on by men, but, his sin being forgiven, he continued in his kingship.[81] Did Peter, who denied Christ three times, not lose savor? And yet, not only did he not lose the apostolate, but he even received the primacy.[82]

Why is it, then, that it says, *If the salt loses its savor, it is good for nothing anymore except to be thrown out, and trodden on by men.* Clearly, it is one thing to lose savor in actions and another to lose savor in beliefs. Whoever loses savor in his actions—as long as he does not lose savor in faith—if he repents, he will always be returned to grace, and often be restored to his [former] status. However, if he loses savor in faith, becoming a heretic or an apostate, he can indeed be returned to grace, but only with difficulty can he be restored to his [former] status, because a scar remains from contracting this kind of leprosy. Peter certainly denied in his words, but not in his heart.

Lest, however, the salt lose its savor in me, which would be destructive and perilous, I ask you, brothers and sons, to implore our most merciful Father with your devout prayers that he himself who admonished blessed Peter, "I have prayed for you, Peter, that your faith will not fail; and you, being converted, confirm your brothers,"[83] may confirm in me, Peter's undeserving and unworthy successor, that faith which works through love,[84] to the glory of his name, to the salvation of my soul, to the strengthening of the universal church, Jesus Christ our Lord, who is over all, blessed God, forever. Amen.

# CONVENING THE FOURTH GENERAL COUNCIL OF THE LATERAN

The Fourth Lateran Council was convened by Pope Innocent III on November 11, 1215. To initiate this great pastoral reform council, he had appropriately chosen a holy day of obligation, the feast of Martin of Tours, a saint highly admired as the "priest of priests," the first bishop-confessor canonized by the western church. For centuries St. Martin had been given the same veneration as the apostles. References to this council often note that it was convened on his feast day. The council opened in the Basilica of St. John (the Baptist) Lateran, the Pope's own church, the administrative center of the papacy, and the mother church of the Christian world. Originally named the Church of the Savior, it was established by Constantine in the year 324. There the Pope himself ordained priests, and it was the setting for the opening ceremonies of Lent and the rites of Maundy Thursday, the commemoration day of the Last Supper. The anniversary of the church's dedication, still observed today as a feast day on the liturgical calendar, had been celebrated only two days before the council opened.[1]

This was to be the apogee of Innocent's brilliant career. At the age of fifty-five Innocent was in his prime, the most influential man in the western world. For eighteen years he had waged moral battles with earthly rulers and had, in many cases, been the victor. His phenomenal energy had carried him into major arenas of public life: political, economic, educational, as well as religious. Now his great plan for the reform of the church was to be put into action. As powerful as he undoubtedly was, however, Innocent knew that to assure the success of his reform he must have the support of his bishops, who were assembled before him now at the pre-dawn Mass in the Lateran Basilica. Innocent himself intoned the hymn "Veni creator spiritus," which was taken up by the assembled prelates, even as great crowds were gathering outside.

This, the twelfth general council in the church's history, was the largest ever held up to that time. "There were present four hundred and four bishops from throughout the western church, and from the Latin eastern church a large number of abbots, canons and representatives of the secular power. No Greeks were present, even those invited, except the patriarch of the Maronites and a legate of the patriarch of Alexandria." There were more than eight hundred abbots and priors, and representatives from cathedrals and collegiate chapters throughout the West. Most Christian rulers were represented, and even the Western Emperor of Constantinople had sent his ambassador. The crowds were so immense that rumors spread of numerous deaths from suffocation, including that of Matthew, Bishop of Amalfi.[2]

The canons of Lateran Council IV were not a surprise to the assembled bishops, for the council had been two and a half years in the planning. In the spring of 1213, Innocent had sent letters calling for the council, and the thirty months of preparation had been time enough for the bishops to become familiar with the reforms Innocent sought.[3]

> To prepare for the forthcoming council during the intervening period the Pope dispatched legates throughout Christendom to investigate abuses to be corrected by conciliar legislation. In a similar manner the bishops were charged to inquire into their dioceses and to submit reports on needed reforms. Robert of Courson's legatine commission stemmed directly from the papal program and his councils held in France prepared for the Lateran Council. As a bishop, Stephen Langton issued synodical statutes for the diocese of Canterbury between July 1213 and July 1214 which anticipated the legislation

of the general council. When the Lateran Council solemnly opened
. . . the careful preparations were in large measure realized.[4]

Therefore, Innocent's rhetorical task in this opening sermon of the
council was not to inform the bishops of his plans, but to inspire
these men with the same sense of mission he himself felt, and to en-
courage them to implement those plans. The bishops must now take
up their responsibilities in assuming "the burden, not only the hon-
or" of leadership.

The text for the council sermon is taken from the words of Christ
to his apostles at the Last Supper, the Passover meal that was to be
the scene of his farewell to them before his passion and death: "I
have desired with longing to eat this Pasch with you before I suffer."[5]
Innocent then makes the words his own by adding "before I die," giving the text a note of personal poignancy.[6] Once again, as in his
coronation sermon, Innocent avoids the Petrine texts, as well as those
for the liturgical season and for the feast day. Instead, he cuts radical-
ly to the central mystery of Christian life and worship, the Paschal
sacrifice of Christ that is perpetuated in the Mass, including the one
which Innocent is now celebrating. From this pivotal event Innocent
claims a context that ranges from the Passover of the Jews, through
the sacrifice of the Cross, to the Supper of the Lamb in the heavenly
Jerusalem, an eschatological world view magnificently illustrated as
the sermon unfolds.[7] The three "passovers" sought by Innocent com-
prise an impressively ambitious program of action. First, he calls for
a new crusade to the Holy Land; then he introduces the standards
and mechanisms for universal church reform; and finally he announces his ultimate goal, the eternal salvation of every human soul.

Because the Fourth Crusade, which had been initiated early in
Innocent's pontificate (1202–4), had been devastated by the political
differences and ambitions among its proponents, it had lost its spiritual motivation without gaining its material objectives. At Lateran
IV, therefore, Innocent III was determined that the idea of crusade
should be returned to its original meaning, i.e., a taking up of the
Cross as a battle standard so that there may be a rescue of the holy
places. As the bishops listened to the Pope's call to arms, they
heard themselves assigned the crusading role of the Maccabees, the

warrior-priests of the Old Testament. Innocent, master of metaphor, chose his figure well: the bishops were to adopt a truly militant stance in their endeavor to "passover" into the Holy Land so as to achieve its rescue.

Innocent's vision of the second and more far-reaching "passover" of church reform goes far beyond the chiding of lax and poorly educated clergymen which had been a characteristic of his pontificate from the beginning.[8] The time for exhortation and disciplining of individuals is past. To stem the tide of heresy threatening the internal integrity of the church a well designed and long sustained effort will be required of all. The Council will now call upon bishops to live up to their names as *episcopi*, "overseers," and "superintendents." Such institutional oversight, or inquisition, was not an innovation.[9] Lateran IV would, however, make it systemic in the church, establishing it as an ongoing policy. Bishops were now to investigate actively, and if necessary to correct, the doctrinal errors being taught by their own clergy. The strong language in Ezekiel's vision of reforming the Aaronide priesthood stresses the urgency of this work. That the later reputation of "inquisition" would make it a synonym for cruelty and brutal intolerance was a contradiction to the call for charity found in the canons of the council,[10] and resulting in outcomes often far different from Innocent's call for a "passover" of the whole people, clergy and laity, into living a full moral, Christian life.[11]

The third *pasch*, the "passing over" to eternal life, is beautifully described in the last section of the sermon by means of an elegant and creative *distinctio*. In it Innocent gives an extensive list of the meanings of the word *mandere*, "to eat," a reminder that he had identified his chief duty as Vicar of Christ to be the feeding of the Lord's household. Once again he claims all Judeo-Christian history as his setting, and recalls directly or by inference all the earlier references to the *Pasch*, leading the listeners' minds and hearts step-by-step from the Passover observance of the Hebrew tradition, through the celebration of the Eucharist, to the heavenly Supper of the Lamb, the final goal of Christian observance and desire. Rather than being a list of miscellaneous lexical and semantic detail, these quotations resonate with each other, echoing the introductory references to the *Pasch*, so that all meanings are carried through to the end of the sermon. The result is an expansion and deepening of the meanings of *Pasch*, transforming the temporal combat to regain the Holy Land and the moral battle of reformation into elements of mankind's eternal struggle to attain heaven.[12] Given the premises of the Christian faith and the meaning of the Catholic priesthood, the historical and spiritual power of the "Passover" figure is the ideal vehicle for accomplishing Innocent's goals, and a splendid theme for a magnificent keynote discourse opening Lateran Council IV.

## CONVENING THE FOURTH GENERAL COUNCIL OF THE LATERAN

*I have desired with longing to eat this Pasch with you before I suffer*, that is, before I die.[13]

Since "for me, to live is Christ, and to die is gain," I do not refuse, if it is ordained by God, to drink the chalice of suffering,[14] whether it will be given to me to drink for the defense of the Catholic faith, or for the aid of the Holy Land, or for the welfare of ecclesiastical liberty. Although I desire to remain in the flesh until the work I have undertaken is finished, nevertheless not mine, but the will of God be done.[15] And so I have said to you, *I have desired with longing to eat this pasch with you, before I suffer*.

The desires of mankind are many and varied: can anyone explain them? But all of them can be reduced to these two: clearly the spiritual and the carnal; the spiritual, which are concerned with celestial and eternal things; and the carnal, concerned with temporal and earthly things. Of the first the Prophet says in a Psalm, "My soul is ravished with desire for your judgments always;"[16] and the Bride says in the Song, "I sat under the shadow of the one I desired, and his fruit was sweet on my tongue."[17] The Apostle (Peter) says of the second, "Flee the desires of the flesh, which war against the spirit,"[18] and another (Ben-Sira), "Remove the desire for evil far away from me."[19] I, however, call upon his testimony who is the steadfast witness in heaven that *I have desired with longing to eat this pasch with you*, not with carnal, but *with* spiritual *desire*; not for earthly profit or temporal glory, but for the reformation of the universal church, and especially for the liberation of the Holy Land. It is chiefly and principally for these two undertakings that I have convened this sacred council.

But perhaps you will say, "What is this *pasch* that you desire to eat with us?" For *pasch* is interpreted in different ways in divine Scripture: as a day—whence, "Now the feast day of unleavened bread, which is called the *pasch*, had drawn nigh";[20] as an hour—whence, "The fourteenth day, toward evening, is the *pasch* of the Lord";[21] as a lamb—whence, "the day of the unleavened bread came, on which the *pasch* must be sacrificed";[22] as unleavened bread—whence, "They did not go into the praetorium so they would not be contaminated, but could eat the *pasch*";[23] as a festival—whence, "before the feast day of the *Pasch*, Jesus knowing that his hour had come, that he might pass from this world to the Father";[24] and even for Christ himself—whence, "Christ our *Pasch* is sacrificed."[25] Indeed *Pasch* in Hebrew is *phase*, which is a "pass(ing) over," and in Greek is *paschein*, which is "to suffer," because it is through suffering we must pass over to glory, as Truth himself said, "It was necessary for the Christ to suffer so as to enter into his glory."[26] For that reason if we wish to co-reign [with him], it is necessary that we also co-suffer [with him], although "the sufferings of this time are not wholly worthy of the future glory that will be revealed in us."[27] This *pasch*, which is the *phase*, that is, "passing over," *I have desired with longing to eat with you*. Of this it is said in Exodus, "They shall eat hastily; for it is the *phase*, that is, the passing over of the Lord."[28]

It is clearly written in the Book of Kings, and very clearly confirmed in Paralipomenon [Chronicles], that in the eighteenth year of the reign of King Josiah the temple was restored and the *phase* was celebrated, in such a way as it had not been done in Israel since the days of the judges and the kings.[29] Let this history of past events be a parable for today's urgent time, so that "in" this "the eighteenth year" of our pontificate[30] "the temple of the Lord," which is the church, may "be restored, and *phase*," or *pasch*, that is this solemn council, "be celebrated." Through this [*pasch*] may there occur among the Christian people, who see God through faith, a true passing over from vices to virtues "in such a way as" in truth "has not occurred in Israel since the days of the judges and the kings," that is, from the times of the Holy Fathers and of the Catholic princes. And I confidently hope in him who makes a promise to his faithful ones, saying, "Wherever two or three are gathered together in my name, I am there among them."[31] He himself is present here to celebrate this Pasch among us who have gathered in this Basilica of the Savior, in the name of the Savior, for those things that pertain to salvation.

Even more, there is a triple *pasch* or *phase* I desire to celebrate with you, physical, spiritual, eternal: physical, so there may be a passing over to a place—to liberate pitiable Jerusalem; spiritual, so there may be a passing over from one condition to another—to reform the universal church;[32] eternal, so there may be a passing over from [earthly] life to [eternal] life—so as to obtain celestial glory.

In the Lamentations of Jeremiah Jerusalem pitiably cries out to us for the physical passover,

"O all you who pass along the way, listen, and see if there is any sorrow like my sorrow. Then pass over to me, all you who love me, so you can free me from my great misery. For I, who used to be the mistress of nations, have now been made a slave; I who used to be crowded with people, now sit as if I were alone. The streets of Sion mourn, because there is no one who comes to the solemn feast. Her enemies have become her lords,"[33] the holy places are all profaned, and the sepulcher of the Lord which used to be revered, is now defiled. Where Jesus Christ the only begotten Son of God was adored, Mohammed, the son of perdition is now worshipped. The alien's sons insult me, and they taunt the wood of the Cross, saying, "You trusted in the wood, now let us see if it can help you." O what shame, what chaos, what ignominy, that the sons of the slave woman, the unworthy

Agarenes,[34] now hold our mother enslaved, the mother of all the faithful, of whom the Psalmist surely speaks, "Mother Sion," he says, "'Everyone is born in her, and the Most High himself has founded her.'" It is there that God our King, before all the ages, chose to accomplish our salvation in the midst of the world.

So what are we to do? Behold, beloved brothers, I wholly commit myself to you; I make myself totally accessible to you. In compliance with your conciliar decision, if you think it expedient, I am prepared personally to undertake this work. I will "pass over" to kings, and princes, and peoples, and nations—and indeed even beyond, to arouse them with a mighty cry—so they will rise up to fight the fight of the Lord and redress the injury of the Crucified One. Because of our sins he was cast out of his land, and from his throne, which he had purchased with his blood, and in which he consummated the whole mystery of our redemption. Regardless of what others may do, we, the priests of the Lord, must especially take up this task, aiding and supporting with personnel and goods the needs of the Holy Land. No one at all should be left who does not participate in such a great work, lest he be deprived of such a great reward. In the past in a similar case, God achieved liberation in Israel through priests, when through the Maccabees, unquestionably priests, the sons of Mattathias, he freed Jerusalem and the temple from ungodly hands.[35]

Now as to the spiritual passover the Lord said "to the man dressed in linen, who had the ink-horn of a scribe at his loins, 'Pass through the center of the city and mark *Tau* on the foreheads of the men who sigh and mourn over all the abominations being committed within it.'"[36] Then he said to the six men who had the weapons of destruction in their hands, "Pass through the city following him, and pierce through and through all on whom you do not find the *Tau*. Let your eye spare no one, and begin at my sanctuary!"[37]

The "man dressed in linen, who had the ink-horn of a scribe at his loins," should be the preacher—a man robust in virtue like the man of whom the Scripture says, "There was a man in the land of Uz, named Job. This man was blameless and upright, fearing God and shunning evil."[38] "Dressed in linen," that is, dressed with honest habits and good works, as is said in another place, "Always see that your garments are dazzling white";[39] that is, let your works be pure. For the "linen" from which the priestly vestments were made, according to the Law, designates cleanliness and honesty because of the radiance to which it is brought by maceration of the flesh, and by contrition.[40] The "scribe," preeminent and supreme, is the Holy Spirit, the finger of God, who wrote the tablets of the Testament. Of him the Psalmist says, "My tongue is the pen of a scribe writing swiftly."[41] The "ink-horn" of this scribe is the gift of knowledge from which the "ink" of doctrine is brought forth by the "pen" of the tongue to be written on the parchment of the heart. The "loins" are the center of our desires. So the Lord commands, "Gird your loins,"[42] and the Psalmist prayed to the Lord, "Purge my loins and my heart."[43] This all means that he who has "the ink-horn of a scribe" is the one who, by the gift of knowledge given him by the Holy Spirit, restrains and moderates the desires of the flesh in himself so that his way of life is not discordant with his teaching, lest it will be said to him, "Physician, heal yourself;"[44] "You who preach that men must not steal, steal; you who teach that men should not commit adultery, commit adultery."[45] So Truth says, "Let your loins be girded up and your lamps burning in your hands."[46]

This man is ordered to "pass through the center of the city and mark *Tau* on the foreheads of the men who sigh and mourn." *T* is the last letter of the Hebrew alphabet, representing the shape of the cross. It was so constituted before Pilate set the inscription above the crucified Lord,[47] and also which the blood of the lamb, smeared on every doorpost and also on the lintels of the houses, mysteriously signified.[48] Whoever by his actions reflects the righteousness of the cross bears this sign on his forehead, just as the Apostle says, "Let him crucify his flesh with its vices and desires,"[49] and thereby let him say with the Apostle, "Far be it from me to glory except in the cross of our Lord Jesus Christ by which the world is crucified to me, and I to the world."[50] Such men certainly sigh and mourn "over all the abominations that are" committed "within" the city. The sins of their neighbors are the frying pans for [searing] the just: "Who," says the Apostle, "is weak and I am not weakened, who is scandalized and I do not burn?"[51]

Just as "the man dressed in linen, who had the ink-horn of a scribe at his loins, should pass through the center of the city and mark *Tau* on the foreheads of the men who sigh and mourn over all the abominations that are committed within it," so the High Priest, who has been constituted watchman[52] over the house of Israel, should pass through the whole church—which is the city of the great King, the city set on a mountain[53]—investigating and inquiring into the merits of individuals,[54] to see whether "they are saying that good is evil or evil good; lest they are judging darkness to be light or light darkness;"[55] lest "they are killing souls that are not dying, or giving life to souls that should not live."[56] It is so that he can distinguish and discern between the one and the other that he should mark *Tau* on the foreheads of the men who mourn. It is to show the ones who "sigh and mourn over the abominations that are committed within" the church that he marks *Tau* on their foreheads. They are the ones who truly "sigh" for the crimes and "mourn" for the disgrace "over the abominations" that are committed " within the the city," because the abomination has already advanced so far that the disgrace is a crime and the crime is a disgrace. So, if we resolutely dig through the wall, as the prophet was commanded to do, we will see worse "abominations," and even the worst "abominations," which have been committed even within the temple.[57]

The "six men," every single one having the weapons of destruction in his hand, should be you men of virtue. There are "six" because of the mystery of that number, so that you will be perfect in word and work; for six is the perfect number, because its sum is drawn from its non-fractional parts. So on the sixth day God completed [the creation] of heaven and earth and all their beauties. And when, in the fulness of time, he came into the world, it was in the sixth age, on the sixth day, at the sixth hour, that he redeemed the human race, even as he spoke his six last words from the cross.[58] The weapon of destruction that you should hold in your hands for punishing the wicked is pontifical authority, which you should wield in your work of vanquishing evildoers.[59] For example, the Psalmist says, "In the morning I killed all the sinners in the land, so that I might cut off all workers of iniquity from the city of the Lord."[60] It is said elsewhere of these weapons, "He has bent his bow and readied it; in it he has armed the weapons of death; he has made his arrows into burning spears."[61] It is therefore commanded you, "Pass over through the center of the city, following him,"—that is, the high priest, as a leader, a prince, and a teacher—so that you "pierce," to whatever degree the fault will require, by interdicting and disbarring, by excommunicating and deposing "all on whom you do not find the *Tau*" marked by him who "closes, and no one opens; who opens, and no one closes."[62] Those marked [with the *Tau*] are not to be harmed, just as it is said elsewhere, "Do not harm the earth, nor the sea, nor the trees until we mark the servants of our God on their foreheads."[63]

As to the others, however, it is said, "Let your eye spare no one,"[64] so that there will be no partiality toward any person[65] among you. Remember what Moses is recorded as having spoken to the sons of Levi, "If any man is the Lord's, let him be joined to me. Let every man put his sword upon his thigh: go out and back and forth from gate to gate through the middle of the camp, and every man kill his brother, and his friend, and his neighbor. And the sons of Levi carried out the command of Moses."[66] May you henceforth similarly carry it out: so strike, that you heal; slay, that you may give life, by the example of him who said, "I will kill and I will give life; I will strike, and I will heal."[67] "And," he said, "at my sanctuary begin!"[68]

Indeed, "It is time," as the blessed Apostle said, "for judgment to begin at the house of the Lord."[69] For all corruption in the people comes first from the clergy, because "If the priest, who is anointed, sins, he makes the people guilty."[70] It is certain that when the laity, see [the clergy] sinning shamelessly and outrageously, they also will fall into sins and ungodliness because of the [clergy's] example. And when they are reproved by anyone, they immediately make excuses for themselves saying, "The Son can do only what he has seen the Father doing,"[71] and "it is enough for the disciple if he is like his master."[72] So this prophecy is fulfilled, "The people will be just like the priest."[73] Indeed now the sea says, "Blush with shame, O Sidon,"[74] for this is where evils have come into the Christian people: faith decays, religion grows deformed, liberty is thwarted, justice is trampled underfoot, heretics emerge, schismatics grow haughty, the faithless rage, the Agarenes conquer.

As to the everlasting Passover the Lord [says], "Blessed are those servants, whom, when the Lord comes, he shall find watching. Truly I say to you, that he will gird himself, and make them sit down to eat, and passing among them he will serve them."[75] About this "passing over" the martyrs rightly rejoice, saying in the Psalm, "We have passed over through fire and water and You have led us into a place of refreshment."[76] This *pasch* above all *I desire to eat with you* in the Kingdom of God. This eating may be physical or spiritual. Of the one it is said, "Give them something to eat;"[77] of the other, "Kill and eat."[78] There is also an eating that is sin and an eating that is punishment. Of the first it is said, "They ate the sacrifices of the dead;"[79] of the other, "My sword shall eat flesh."[80] There is also the eating that is doctrine and the eating that is penitence. Of the first it is said, "I have food to eat that you do not know;"[81] of the other, "They ate ashes like bread."[82] Moreover, there is the eating of the Eucharist, and the eating that is eternal glory. Of the Eucharist it is said, "He that eats me shall live because of me;"[83] of eternal glory it is written, "Blessed is he who will eat bread in the kingdom of God."[84]

It is especially in this final eating that *I long with desire to eat this pasch with you* so that we may pass from labor to rest, from sorrow to joy, from unhappiness to glory, from death to life, from corruption to eternity, our Lord Jesus Christ granting it, to whom is honor and glory forever. Amen.

# IN SYNOD

Once again addressing his clergy in synod, Innocent now unfolds his ascetical theology of Holy Orders within the powerful historic and poetic setting of Psalm Sixty-seven (LXX numeration). Even today this remains "widely admitted as textually and exegetically the most difficult and obscure of all the psalms."[1] Medieval exegetes recognized lexical, grammatical, and syntactical problems within the text, but were able to accommodate them within their interpretation of all the psalms as prophetic of Christ as the centripetal point who gives meaning to sacred history by drawing all things to himself.[2] Historically Psalm Sixty-seven is a triumphant celebration of victories: the Exodus, the return of the Ark to Jerusalem, and the "making captivity captive" as celebrated in the Easter liturgy. Here the moral exhortations of Innocent's other sermons are lifted from an admonitory to an inspirational tone. By exploiting the obscurities and multilevel references of the text Innocent expands his idea of priesthood to eternal proportions, commensurate with the eternal significance of the priestly vocation as he understood it.

The superb intricacy of Innocent's rhetorical power reaches its culmination in this sermon. The complexity with which he weaves the allusions, scriptural overtones, and etymological resonances of his argument defy discrete analysis. Moreover, within the sermon the pericope is rendered not only in the Vulgate translation, but also in the Greek idiom, so that it is given two different, although complementary, readings. This unusual device enables Innocent to display every facet of each word's meaning so as to produce a richly textured exegesis. For example, he presents all the varied meanings of the word *cleros:* as a patrimony or inheritance, a (p)lot of ground, a lot in life, a portion or share, even a legal claim made by those who are at once cut off from the people by reason of being chosen and set apart from the others, yet pledged to the service of the people by that very choice. The identification of the clergy as "chosen" derives from God's original separation of the Levites from the rest of the Israelites so they could be his ministers.[3] Since their duties left no time for earning a livelihood, they received no portion of real property. Their "portion," or share of the inheritance, was God himself, the priesthood, and its requisites.[4] God in turn claimed the Israelites, whom he had chosen from all other tribes, as his portion or inheritance.[5] To the extent that God can be "chosen" by those entering the clergy, he becomes their "lot": that is, by choosing him they necessarily exclude secular choices which are outside the boundaries of their "portion."[6] All these levels of meaning work together in Innocent's understanding of what it means to be "clergy."[7]

Similarly he develops the meaning of *inter* as "being among" or "between." Here he has made use of Peter Lombard's work, based on Augustine's longer commentary on Psalm 67. Peter notes that the Greek construction gives *inter* the meaning of an intimate bond based on consent between partners in an agreement: in Latin "between me and you," and in Greek " I will put my covenant in the middle of me and you." This distinction emphasizes the priesthood in its intermediary role, as well as stressing the unity which should exist among the presbyterium.

This image of "clergy" is presented poetically in the figure of the dove with silvered wings and golden pinions. As the dove is the church, so are the clergy its wings, *pennae,* derived from *petere,* "to seek."[8] These "seeking-wings" impart to the figure a powerful sense of eagerness, of rushing and soaring heavenward. Added to these synchronous meanings of the recurring terms is the representation of the dove as hovering between heaven and earth, once again illustrating the necessary tension of the intermediaries interceding between God and those individual souls living in worldly circumstances.

It is in the *distinctio* of the word *medios,* "intermediary," that Innocent brings to bear the subtleties of scholastic method on the unfolding of the existential paradoxes of the priestly life, the dissonance he himself experienced as mediator between the secular and spiritual dimensions of his office. As intercessors and intermediaries the priests are constituted between God and the world. At every moment they must provide balance between these two poles. Theirs is not the median balance of classical "moderation," but the precarious, practical, and critical tension of making the middle "hold." Innocent encapsulates this complex understanding of the clergy and its work in an unusual figure of speech that links the tasks of the Levitical priesthood (Exodus 26:1–11) with the Gospel commissioning of the Apostles (Matthew 5:16) and with the apocalyptic Second Coming of Christ (Revelation 22:17):

> "Therefore let your light shine before men so that they may see your good works and glorify your Father in heaven," just as "one curtain draws another curtain" and "He who hears, let him say, 'Come.'"

The "curtain" refers to the duties of Levites, who during the desert wanderings and until the Temple was built in Jerusalem assembled the moveable Tabernacle, which housed the innermost Tent of Meeting, where the Ark of the Covenant was kept. They were instructed to work together to enclose the Tabernacle by hoisting the heavy draperies of the covering into place on rods, each curtain pulling the next into place. Completed, the Tent of Meeting became the Dwelling Place of the Lord, whose presence resided there. In the same way, Innocent suggests, when the clergy's work of drawing the world to the faith is completed, Christ will come, and the faithful clergy may then soar into the glory they have merited, carrying the church aloft to God. It is with this promise that Innocent concludes his instruction to his clerical brethren, joining his own hope with theirs that they may together achieve the rewards of their labors.

## IN SYNOD

*If you sleep among the chosen mediators, you will be like the silvered wings of the dove, and her back pinions splendid in gold.*[9]

For us (the clergy), two things are necessary if we wish to merit our inheritance: specifically, [our] lives, and [our] teaching. The first is in our own behalf, the other is for our neighbors. For "Jesus set out to teach and to do . . . leaving us an example, that we might follow in his footsteps. He did not commit sin, nor was deceit found in his mouth."[10] Because "He did not commit sin," there was honesty in his life; "nor was deceit found in his mouth," and so there was truth in his teaching.

These two [duties] are entrusted to us in these words: *If you sleep* is stated first and about our lives; *among the chosen mediators* is then added, about our teaching. This is why pomegranates hung with golden bells from the High Priest's vestment.[11] The "pomegranates" represent religious service;[12] the "golden bells" symbolize preaching. These two [duties] must be conjoined in the priest, lest "entering the sanctuary without them, he will die."[13]

Since through merit the reward is attained, rightly the promised reward follows upon merit. What is promised is twofold: one [reward] in the present, the other in the future. Devotion to duty[14] carries with it a promise for our life in the present, where it receives a hundred-fold, as well as in the future, where it will possess eternal life: a hundred-fold in the present, life eternal in the future. *Silvered wings of the dove,* refers to the present; *and her back pinions splendid in gold,* refers to the future. "Because God loves mercy and truth: the Lord will give grace and glory."[15] "Grace" he awards for merit in the present; he will bestow "glory" in the future as a reward.

There are also two kinds of *sleep:* one the sleep of death, the other the sleep of life. Again, each of these is of two kinds. One *sleep* of death is bodily, which is a punishment; the other is the *sleep* of spiritual death, and this is sin.[16] Of the first the Lord said to the Apostles, "Our friend Lazarus is asleep,"[17] and the Apostle

(Paul) said, "I will not have you ignorant about those who are asleep, [so that you will not be sorrowful, like others who have no hope]."[18] Of the second David said, "Can he who sleeps throw it off and rise again?"[19] And the Apostle (Paul) said, "Awake, you who sleep. Arise from among the dead, and Christ will give you light."[20] This can be understood in three ways: in ignorance, in negligence, and in concupiscence. The Psalmist speaks of the *sleep* of ignorance, "Enlighten my eyes so I may never fall asleep in death."[21] Solomon speaks of the *sleep* of negligence, "How long can you sleep, you sluggard? When will you awaken from your sleep? You will sleep a little, you will drowse a little, you will fold your hands a little so you can sleep, and destitution will overtake you like a bandit, and poverty [will attack you] like an armed brigand."[22] David says about the *sleep* of concupiscence, "They slept their sleep, all the men of riches, and they found nothing in their hands."[23]

We also read in the Scriptures about the twofold *sleep* of life: the sleep of bodily life arising from nature, and the other, of the spiritual life, sleep resulting from grace. The Lord said to the Apostles about natural slumber, "Sleep now and rest."[24] Of the second the Spouse said in the Canticle, "I sleep, and my heart is watchful."[25] So we also, dearly beloved, must be watchful as we are *asleep*, asleep to evils, even as we are vigilant in goodness.

It is certain that the perfection[26] of life consists of two actions: rejecting vice and practicing virtue. As Scripture says, "Renounce evil and do good,"[27]—so that by the first we can avoid punishment, and by the second we can win the prize. Both of these actions are easily understood through [the image of] "sleep." *Sleep*, as those who explain natural things assert, is the dormancy of our souls' power as our natural functions intensify.[28] However, we, who are spiritual, can find these powers spiritually in our souls. There are in fact three natural powers in the soul: the power of reason, the power of desire, the power of anger. Reason is, as it were, a digestive power, because it discerns between good and evil, between light and darkness, between the holy and the profane. Desire is like an appetitive power, because it chooses good, eagerly seeks the light, pursues what is holy. Anger is like an excretory power, because it drives out evil, repels darkness, and spits out the unholy. By contrast, there are three human weaknesses in the soul: ignorance, negligence, and concupiscence. Ignorance is opposed to reason. Negligence is opposed to anger. Concupiscence is opposed to desire. It is above all in regard to these three vices that we need to be *asleep*, because our faults result from our negligence, and our sins result from our concupiscence, while from ignorance the results are both faults and sins. There is a difference between a fault and a sin: a fault consists in omission, sin in commission. Not doing what should be done is a fault; sin is doing what should not be done.

So we should be *asleep* to ignorance, especially ignorance of the commandments, in the divine precepts, and also of our duties in regard to the ecclesiastical sacraments—the two things we cannot ignore without peril.[29] For it is written, "They would not learn my ways; so I swore to them in my wrath that they would not enter into my peace."[30] "Those who walked in darkness neither knew nor understood."[31] The Lord said through the Prophet, "You have rejected knowledge, so I will reject you lest you administer the priestly office for me."[32] "And my nation was led away captive, because it was ignorant. Its aristocracy perished in hunger, and its people withered with thirst."[33] "He did not wish to learn how to do good works. He has plotted wickedness even in his bed."[34] "If they had only known, they would never have crucified the Lord of glory."[35]

We must be especially wary of ignorance, we to whom it has been given *ex officio* to understand the mysteries of the kingdom of God—while to others they were given only in parables.[36] We must be the "oxen plowing," while others are the "asses grazing near by."[37] For when we sing to God we [daily] promise anew, "I will meditate upon Your laws, I will not forget Your words."[38] We should be the light of the world.[39] "But, if the light within us becomes darkness, how great will the darkness itself be!"[40] We should be the salt of the earth: "If the salt loses its savor, how can it (the earth) be salted? The salt is good for nothing any more but to be thrown out, and trampled on by men."[41] Therefore, let your ignorance sleep, and your reason guide you, as: "Your service must be reasonable,"[42] and, "Be prepared, if anyone asks you, to give an explanation of this faith that is in you."[43]

This knowledge then is the *logion* or *rationale* which the High Priest wore on his breast. On it was written *Urim* and *Thummim*, that is, Manifestation and Truth.[44] For in the breast of the priest the knowledge of truth should be manifested as in the prophecy: "The lips of the priest safeguard knowledge, and the people expect the Law from his mouth, because he is the messenger of the Lord of hosts."[45] The *rationale* was a quadrangle, because the priest must discern among four things: between the true and the false, lest he err in his belief; between good and evil, lest he err in his actions. [The *rationale*] was also double, just as the priest must discern doubly: for himself and for the people, lest "If the blind lead the blind, they will both fall into the pit."[46] So we should be asleep to ignorance, because "He who guards Israel will neither slumber nor sleep."[47] He will not slumber in regard to our punishment, unless we *sleep* in regard to our sinning.

We should be *asleep* also to negligence, particularly in prayer, which is giving attention to the Lord, and also in disciplining, which requires that we give attention to our neighbor. We can neglect neither of these without sinning. Some pray so negligently and undevotedly that they are saying heavenly things with their mouths while their hearts are thinking of earthly things. The Lord reproaches them through the Prophet (Isaiah), "This people honors me with their lips, but their hearts are far from me."[48] Of such it is read, "They were blessing with their mouth, but cursing in their heart."[49] Those "bless with their mouth" who speak the eloquence of truth; but they "curse in their heart" who occupy their minds with the emptiness of vanity. Others pray so quickly and casually, that, the middle of the prayer having been skipped over, they produce nothing but its head and its tail! But how can God hear clearly someone who cannot hear his own self? Whoever prays in that way does not incline God to granting favors, but rather provokes him to wrath. "But you, when you pray, go into your bedchamber, and having shut the door, pray to your Father."[50] "Go into the bedchamber" of your heart, "the door" of the senses "having been closed," lest the "dying flies spoil the sweetness of the perfume."[51] Pray to your Father not in talkativeness, as heathens do. They think they will be heard by much talking,[52] Rather [pray] "in a pure heart and a good conscience, and a genuine faith."[53] This is the way Moses and Susanna prayed. They cried out to the Lord, and he freed them from their needs.[54] They cried out, not so much by straining their voices, as with the devotion of their hearts. As the Psalmist says, "Take delight in the Lord and he will grant the prayers of your heart."[55] The Apostle (Paul) also says, "Sing and make music in your hearts."[56] For God is the listener not so much to the voice, as to the heart. Nor is he persuaded by shouting, "he who is the searcher of desires and hearts."[57] Anna, portraying an image of the church, can be seen to have obeyed this [precept]. She obtained what she sought, not by loud demands, but by dedicated prayer. It is written in the Book of Kings: "Anna spoke within her heart, while only her lips moved, and her voice could not be heard at all."[58] Whence in the Psalm, "Be sorry in your beds for the things you have said in your hearts,"[59] because "A repentant soul is a sacrifice to God; a contrite and humble heart God will not despise."[60]

Even so, it is helpful that saying the prayers aloud should be combined with devout emotion, because, like a breath blown on charcoal, expression engenders devotion. Listen to what the Psalmist says about this: "I cried out to him with my mouth; I praised him with my tongue."[61] You, therefore, dear friends, when you pray, stand before the Lord our God remorseful, humble, and devout, without movement, without laughter, without scoffing. Do not shout too much or hurry too much. Pronounce distinctly so as to be understood, because "The man who does the work of God negligently is cursed."[62] Therefore, "serve the Lord in fear and praise him with trembling,"[63] especially in the sacrifice in which the memorial of the death of Christ is celebrated. "Do this," he said, "in my memory."[64] And the Apostle (Paul) said, "As often as you eat this bread and drink this cup, you proclaim the death of the Lord until he comes."[65] Negligence in any duty is sin, but in the sacrifice it is perilous, because "He who eats unworthily, eats a judgment on himself, not discerning the body of the Lord."[66]

Let us also beware of negligence in the correction of sinners. Some [priests] are "silent dogs, not strong enough to bark,"[67] flattering the vices of sinners, either from avaricious desire, or from weak timidity—from avaricious desire, lest by chance they may lose offerings or tithes; from weak timidity, lest by chance they may incur disapproval or hatred. Against such as these it is said by the Prophet (Ezekiel), "Woe to those who sew cushions to put under every elbow and make pillows for the heads of those of all ages."[68] Also, "Some were indeed building the wall, but others were merely daubing over it again."[69] "Your prophets predicted silly and deceptive things for you. They were not exposing your sin to you, so as to call you out to repentance."[70] To the contrary it is commanded, "Cry out, cease not, lift up your voice like a trumpet, and proclaim to my people their crimes, and to the house of Jacob their sins."[71] So the Apostle (Paul) said to the Ephesians, "My hands are clean of all your blood, for I have not flinched from proclaiming to you all the counsels of God."[72] Hear the Prophet (Isaiah), "Woe to me because I have been silent, because I am a man of unclean lips and I live amid a people of unclean lips."[73] John did not fear Herod, boldly reproaching him because he had taken Herodias as his wife, while her husband, Philip, was alive.[74]

Let negligence sleep, therefore, and let anger be aroused, as in "Be angry and sin not."[75] That is, be angry at vices lest you sin. This is the zeal with which Christ was inflamed when he drove the sellers and buyers from the temple as, "The zeal of your house has eaten me up."[76] [This was the zeal] in which Phineas, enraged, transfixed the Israelite with a lance when he had gone in to the Midianite.[77] In this way the discerning priest exercises severity against rebels and the obstinate, while showing compassion towards the humble and penitent. Do not imitate the man who had been left wounded, half-dead, half-alive, and whom the Samaritan took into the inn, and poured wine and oil over.[78] Before the ark of the tabernacle [Aaron's] rod and the manna were kept side by side.[79]

We must be *asleep* also to all concupiscence, particularly to the desire for the things proceeding from avarice, and to that desire for women which comes from licentiousness. For it is written, "Nothing is more wicked than the covetous man, and nothing more sinful than to love money."[80] This is the word of the wise man (Sirach)[81] confirmed by the Apostle (Paul) saying, "They who wish to become rich fall into temptation and into the snare of the devil, and into many useless and harmful desires, that plunge men into destruction and perdition, because the root of all evils is avarice."[82] Elsewhere he says, "Avarice is the serving of idols."[83] Hear what the Prophet (Micah) says against covetous priests, "Her princes were pronouncing judgments for bribes, and her priests gave instruction for wages, and her prophets divined for money."[84] "Hell and perdition are bottomless; and likewise the eyes of men are insatiable."[85] There are two "daughters of the leech" who say, "Give [to me], give [to me]."[86] "For the love of money grows, even as the money itself increases."[87] "Yet the world passes away, and its concupiscence."[88] "We must not fear it when a man becomes rich, and the glory of his house is increased. When he dies he cannot take away any of it; nor can his glory go down with him."[89] I do not say that one may not have riches, but that it is very wrong to cling to riches, as in "Even if your riches overflow, do not set your heart [on them]."[90] For that reason no one of you should take over another's parishioner, or go into another's parish. It is a precept that no one may send a sickle into another's harvest,[91] nor cross the boundaries which our fathers set.

Let us be no less on guard against the desire for women, for "Wine and women make wise men desert their faith," and because of women's beauty many perish.[92] "Her houses are roads to hell, penetrating into the inner chambers of death."[93] Always Ardor and Wantonness precede her, always Foulness and Uncleanness accompany her, always Sorrow and Regret follow her. "For the lips of a harlot taste like a honeycomb dripping, and her throat is smoother than oil, but her aftertaste is bitter as wormwood and sharp as a two-edged sword."[94] The enemy is an intimate friend, living not far away but close by. He is not outside but within, for "His power is in his loins and his strength in the navel of his belly."[95] He is never escaped, unless he is fled; he is never slain, unless he is first weakened.[96] Moreover, we, constituted in holy orders, are necessarily obliged to guard chastity. For it is written that when David fled the persecution of Saul, he came into Nob to Ahimelech the priest, asking that five loaves be given him to drive out hunger. The priest replied, "I have no unconsecrated bread at hand, but only holy bread. If the young men are clean, especially from women, they may eat it."[97] He did not say, if they have faith, hope, and charity; if they have justice, fortitude, prudence, and temperance; if they have the spirit of wisdom and understanding, the spirit of counsel and fortitude, the spirit of knowledge and piety, and the spirit of fear of the Lord.[98] But he said, "If they are clean, especially from women, they may eat it," since they can not eat the holy bread worthily unless they are clean from sexual union with women.

Let concupiscence go to *sleep*, therefore, and then let your whole desire burst into flames, as "My soul has desired to long for your laws always."[99] And let your desire be kindled by the three principal virtues, faith, hope, and charity. Let your reason be illumined by faith, your anger strengthened by hope, and your desire enlightened by charity. Let your desire be illumined by the truth of faith so that reason can expel the errors of ignorance. Let it be strength-

ened by the firmness of hope so that anger can drive out the slug-
gishness of negligence. Let it be shaped by the perfection of charity so that true desire may extinguish the fever of concupiscence.

Finally, let us *sleep among the chosen mediators*. That is, as in the
Greek, we are "at the median point that is the clergy." Literally, we
live *among the chosen mediators* for the whole world. Because of our position, therefore, our actions, whether they be good or bad, cannot
be hidden. "Therefore, let your light shine before men so that they
may see your good works, and glorify your Father who is in heav-
en."[100] In just that way one curtain draws another, and "He who
hears, will say, 'Come.'"[101]

We can also understand this in another way. κλῆρος is interpreted "lot" or "inheritance." That is why they are called *clergy*, they
are chosen by lot as the Lord's portion, as in, "The Lord is the
portion of my inheritance."[102] This inheritance is, moreover, a
triple legacy: low, middle, and high. The "low" inheritance is earthly, as is written, "He gave them their land as an inheritance, an inheritance for Israel his servant."[103] The "middle" one is Sacred
Scripture, of which it is said, "I have inherited your words as a
legacy forever, because they are the joy of my heart."[104] The "high"
inheritance is heavenly beatitude, as it is written, "The boundary
lines of my share have fallen in very beautiful places; to me my inheritance is magnificent."[105] Each of these legacies has its own median: as to earthly possessions, [the median is between] changeable
things and those that never change; in Sacred Scripture, [the median is between] the spirit and the letter; in heavenly beatitude, [it is
between] the vestment of the mind and that of the body.

*Among* these *chosen mediators, between* those median *inheritances*, we
must sleep, differently for each. For there is a median that touches
on both extremes; there is a median that touches neither extreme;
and there is one that touches on only one of two extremes. For example, a median touching both extremes is air, which is midmost
between heaven and earth, and touches both. A median touching
neither extreme is the sun, which is midway between heaven and

earth, and touches neither. A median touching only one of two extremes is the tree which is midmost between heaven and earth, and touches only one. It is in this way, *among* these *chosen mediators*, and *between* these *inheritances*, that we must *sleep*.

Let us *sleep*, therefore, *between the inheritances* of earthly possessions, with the power of anger, so that we rest in neither portion, as is written, "Little children, do not love the world, nor the things that are in the world."[106] Let us *sleep between the inheritances* of Sacred Scripture with the power of reason, so that we rest only in one part, as is written, "The letter kills, but the spirit gives life."[107] Let us sleep *between the inheritances* of heavenly happiness with the power of desire, so that we may rest in both portions, as it is written, "Be glad and rejoice, for your reward is abundant in heaven."[108] Be glad for the vestment of your heart, and rejoice also for the vestment of the body.

If we shall have slept in this way, we will have truly become the *silvered wings of the dove*. As the church is signified by the *dove*, so by the *wings of the dove* the priests of the church are signified, who by their words and example carry her up to heaven. As the spouse said of the bride in the Canticle, "My dove is one, my perfect one."[109] The prophet perfectly described her *wings* when he said, "Who are these who fly like clouds and like doves to their cotes?"[110] The *silvered wings* are those who are learned in divine eloquence, as in, "The words of the Lord, pure words; like silver tried in the fire, purged of the earth, refined seven times."[111] It is said elsewhere, "Your eyes are like doves washed with milk. They rest beside the abundant streams."[112] There are, also *wings* of virtue, *wings* of contemplation, and *wings* of teaching. Of the first is written, "He flew upon the wings of the winds."[113] Of the second, "Who will give me the wings of a dove, and I will fly, so I may be at rest?"[114] Of the third is written, "The wings of each one were joined to the wings of another."[115] However, there are true *wings* and there are false. "True" are the *wings* of the just, represented by the wings of the heron; "false" are the *wings* of hypocrites, represented by the wings of the ostrich. As in Job, "The wing of the ostrich looks like the wing of the heron and of the hawk [but it does not fly]."[116]

Let us be *wings* in flight, looking down on the things of earth with the power of anger, *sleeping between the inheritances* of worldly possessions. Let us be the *wings of a dove* seeking celestial things with the power of desire so we may *sleep between the inheritances* of everlasting happiness. Let us be *silvered wings*, understanding divine things with the power of reason, *sleeping between the inheritances* of Sacred Scripture. Let us in our present life be not only the *silvered wings of the dove*, but also *her back pinions splendid in gold*. The "back" signifies the labor of the present life, as in "Sinners have wrought their works upon my back;"[117] and the *back pinions* represent the restfulness of our future life, as in "Then there will be no more mourning, or crying, or any sorrow; because the former things will have passed away."[118] Therefore, *her back pinions*, that is, the rest after our labor, will be *splendid in gold*, that is, in the glory of contemplation, which is perfectly represented by a golden sheen.[119] For "The just shall shine like the sun in their Father's kingdom."[120] To that glory may the Lord Jesus Christ lead us, he who is God blessed forever. Amen.

# EPILOGUE

In the letter he wrote to his friend Arnald as a prologue to a collection of his sermons, Innocent III said that preaching is the "gate to Paradise." Poetically at least, this was to be true for him. A century after Innocent's death, Dante Alighieri, who righteously condemned more than one pope to the torments of his "Inferno," allowed Innocent's name a place in his "Paradiso."[1] Dante's inclusion of this Pope's name among the citizens of Paradise seems to be based purely on the authorization for preaching that St. Francis of Assisi received from Innocent, a pope whose reputation rests primarily on his role as a powerful political figure dominating the secular world of his time. It is worth consideration that Dante, an astute evaluator of human character, and himself a man deeply involved in political struggles, would see as Innocent's most significant act, not his dealings with kings and heretics, nor his inauguration of crusades and inquisition, but his approval of St. Francis's order of poor preachers.

So many of the august personages with whom Innocent dealt were figures of great power and wealth. In their day they ruled empires, commanded armies, terrified their enemies, and spent their riches not only for personal pleasure, but also to increase their dominance and to intimidate their rivals. Innocent III, himself a man of wealth and power, was quite at ease in this company. Today, however, this lustrous assemblage of historical figures, Innocent III among them, has largely been consigned to the pages of the history books. Few readers now search them out, and then only to study them as medieval characters of mainly academic interest. One of Innocent's contemporaries, however, Francis of Assisi, escapes the dusty tomes and, all these centuries later, cheerfully and benignly invades countless gardens and grottos, farms and festivals, lending his name to cities, churches, hospitals, and religious orders, a living presence effortlessly stealing human hearts with his warmth and humor. For every earnest scholar who seeks out Innocent III on the library shelves, tens of thousands of pilgrims each year make their way to Assisi, so as to feel somehow closer to the "Poverello," and to ask for his intercession with God. There they honor him as they kneel at his tomb in the majestic double basilica which his devotees had built so quickly and so lovingly soon after his death. No such shrine awaited Innocent III. Death overtook the Pope, not in Rome, but in Perugia, the neighboring stronghold and perennial enemy of Assisi.[2] As he lay dying in the hilltop fortress, did Innocent perhaps recall that the little friar had come from the nearby town on the lower slope of Mount Subiaco? Was Francis's home within sight across the plain of Umbria? And what might Francis have thought when he learned that the night after the Pope's death, when his body was lying in state but unguarded, it was stripped of its magnificent and costly papal vestments and left half naked on its bier?[3] Only centuries later would Innocent's bones be discovered, and then ignominiously returned to Rome by train in the suitcase of an unnamed cleric.[4]

The irony of this outcome would not be lost on a man of Innocent's wit, nor would he miss the paradox it sets before us. The contrast between these two apparently incongruous historical figures is on the surface only; their resemblance is clear. Both were men of great charm and magnetism; both led lives of personal virtue and inexhaustible zeal. They shared the sublime vision of "rebuilding the universal church," the goal Innocent set for himself at his consecration, and which he hoped to bring to fruition at the culmination of his life's work, his great Ecumenical Council, Lateran IV.[5] The reforms of that Council, conceived in the mind of the aristocratic Pope, were taken to heart by the merchant's son, who likely was among the throngs in Rome to hear the Council documents proclaimed. Bonaventure tells us that Francis preached on "the Lord's Pasch, that is His passing over from this world to the Father,"[6] and on the Ezekiel text (9:4) of the Lateran IV sermon. He took as his personal signature the *Tau* that Innocent had said must mark the faithful Christian.[7] He went on Crusade as a barefoot knight to convert the Saracens; he was deeply devoted to the Eucharist; and he took up the preacher's life to urge the moral reform so consistently exhorted by Innocent. In fact Francis, a man of "the very greatest faith," lived out both the letter and the spirit of Lateran Council IV. It was not that Francis was a spiritual leader and Innocent was not. Rather, it was Innocent who provided the practical blueprint for Francis's spirituality to follow.

As young men Francis and Lothario had both restored the crumbling church buildings close at hand: Francis at San Damiano in Assisi, Lothario at Sts. Sergius and Bacchus in Rome. Later, when Lothario had become Pope, it is said that he saw Francis in a dream, holding up on his shoulders the great Lateran Basilica, symbol of a more universal church in danger of crashing into ruin. Together, each in his own sphere of influence, each with the talents at his command, the Pope and the poor preacher would seek to rebuild that church. It can be convincingly argued that divine solicitude gave them to one another, and that neither could have had so lasting an imprint on the world without the other. Perhaps Dante, with the wisdom of poets, could see that the two great figures of the time shared the vision of spiritual renewal that informed both their lives. Perhaps, with poetic license, he might also let Innocent share the farewell to Francis: that "his goodly spirit should move forth returning to its appointed kingdom,"[8] *passing over* into Paradise, the home to which Innocent III and Francis of Assisi wished to bring the world.

# ENDNOTES

## Notes to Foreword

1. On the history of preaching, see J. B. Schneyer, *Geschichte der katholischen Predigt* (Freiburg im Breisgau: Seelsorge Verlag, 1968). For the Middle Ages, see B. M. Kienzle, ed., *The Sermon*, Typologie des sources du moyen âge occidental, fasc. 81–83 (Turnhout: Brepols, 2000).

2. There is a growing body of literature on medieval preaching. For bibliography, see Kienzle, *The Sermon*, 19–142; also, Richard and Mary Rouse, *Preachers, Florilegia, and Sermons: Studies on the "Manipulus Florum" of Thomas of Ireland* (Toronto: Pontifical Institute of Mediaeval Studies, 1979); Thomas Amos, Eugene Green, and Beverly Kienzle, eds., *De Ore Domini: Preacher and Word in the Middle Ages* (Kalamazoo: Medieval Institute Publications, Western Michigan University, 1989); Beverly Kienzle, ed., *Models of Holiness in Medieval Sermons: Proceedings of the International Symposium (Kalamazoo, 4–7 May 1995)* (Louvain-la-neuve: Fédération internationale des Instituts d'études médiévales, 1996); Phyllis Roberts, *Studies in the Sermons of Stephen Langton* (Toronto: Pontifical Institute of Mediaeval Studies, 1968); and Augustine Thompson, O.P., *Revival Preachers and Politics in Thirteenth century Italy* (OxfordClarendon Press, 1992).

3. Thomas N. Hall, "The Early Medieval Sermon," in Kienzle, ed., *The Sermon*, 203–47.

4. See the useful discussion in John Howe, *Church Reform and Social Change in Eleventh-Century Italy: Dominic of Sora and his Patrons* (Philadelphia: University of Pennsylvania Press, 1997), 24–57.

5. Giles Constable, *The Reformation of the Twelfth Century* (Cambridge: Cambridge University Press, 1996), 296–328.

6. On crusade preaching, see Penny Cole, *The Preaching of the Crusade to the Holy Land, 1095–1270* (Cambridge, MA: Medieval Academy of America, 1991) and Christoph Maier, *Preaching the Crusades* (Cambridge: Cambridge University Press, 1994) as well as his *Crusade Propaganda and Ideology: Model Sermons for the Preaching of the Cross* (Cambridge: Cambridge University Press, 2000), which contains editions and translations of seventeen crusade sermons.

7. Rouse, *Preachers*, 43–64, provides an excellent summary of the development of preaching in the twelfth and thirteenth centuries. See also the outstanding work of David d'Avray, *The Preaching of the Friars: Sermons Diffused from Paris before 1300* (Oxford: Clarendon Press, 1985), 13–64.

8. John C. Moore, "The Sermons of Pope Innocent III," *Römische historische Mitteilungen* 36 (1994), 81–142, provides a valuable introduction to Innocent's sermons. For the sermons of Honorius III, see my articles, "*Pastor Bonus:* Some Evidence of Honorius III's Use of the Sermons of Pope Innocent III," *Speculum* 52 (1977), 522–37; "The Prefatory Letters to the Sermons of Pope Honorius III and the Reform of Preaching," *Rivista di Storia della Chiesa in Italia* 33 (1979), 95–104; and "Honorius III's 'Sermo in Dedicatione Ecclesie Lateranensis,' and the Historical-Liturgical Traditions of the Lateran," *Archivum Historiae Pontificiae* 21 (1983), 195–209.

9. On vernacular preaching, see Michel Zink, *La Prédication en langue romane: avant 1300* (Paris: H. Champion, 1976).

## Notes to Introduction

1. *Prologus,* PL 217: 309–10.

2. Phyllis B. Roberts, "The Pope and the Preachers: Perceptions of the Religious Role of the Papacy in the Preaching Tradition of the Thirteenth-Century English Church," in *The Religious Roles of the Papacy: Ideals and Realities, 1150–1300,* ed. Christopher Ryan (Toronto: Pontifical Institute of Mediaeval Studies, 1989), 287.

3. Friedrich Kempf, "Innocent III," in Martin Greschat, ed., *Das Papsttum I: Von den Anfängen bis zu den Päpsten in Avignon* (Stuttgart: Verlag W. Kohlhammer, 1985), 196.

4. See James M. Powell, *Innocent III: Vicar of Christ or Lord of the World?,* 2nd ed. (Washington, D.C.: The Catholic University of America Press, 1994).

5. John W. Baldwin, *Masters, Princes, and Merchants: The Social Views of Peter the Chanter and His Circle,* vol. 1 (Princeton: Princeton University Press, 1970), 343. The list of great twelfth-century scholars whose lives and teachings shaped theology in Paris during Innocent's time includes Peter the Lombard, Hugh and Richard of St. Victor, Peter Comester, Peter the Chanter, and Alan of Lille. Wilhelm Imkamp, *Das Kirchenbild Innocenz' III (1198–1216),* Papste und Papsttum 22. (Stuttgart: Hiersemann, 1983), 25–26, discusses Gilbert of Porre, also Peter of Corbeil, with whom Innocent as Pope corresponded.

6. Kenneth Pennington, "The Legal Education of Pope Innocent III," in *Popes, Canonists and Texts, 1150–1550* (Brookfield, Vermont: Variorum, 1993).

7. *Gesta,* PL 214: 80–81.

8. The Roman Curia was and is the bureaucracy that assists the Pope in administering the business of the church. It was constituted in its present form in 1150. It includes the chancery, the treasury, and other offices and tribunals headed by the Cardinals, who were originally pastors of the churches of Rome, pastorates that are now almost entirely titular. The Dean of the College of Cardinals is the Bishop of Ostia.

9. Richard Krautheimer, *Rome: Profile of a City 312–1308,* 2nd rev. ed. (Princeton: Princeton University Press, 1980), 81–82.

10. These three works are available in PL 217 and will be cited as *De miseria, De mysteriis,* and *De quad.* For the title *De missarum mysteriis,* see Michele Maccarrone, "Innocenzo III teologo della eucarista," in *Studi sull'Innocento III* (Padua, 1972), 344–45.

For recent editions, see Robert E. Lewis, ed., *Lothario dei Segni (Pope Innocent III), De miseria condicionis humane* (Athens, GA: University of Georgia Press, 1978); Connie Mae Munk, *A Study of Pope Innocent III's Treatise "De quadripartita specie nuptiarum,"* 2 vols. (Dissertation, University of Kansas; Ann Arbor, Michigan: University Microfilms, 1975). There is no modern edition of *De mysteriis.* Innocent composed a fourth treatise, *Commentarium in septem psalmos penitentiales,* PL 217: 967–1130 (hereafter cited as *In septem psalmos*), which according to MS Vat. lat. 699, reported by Imkamp, *Kirchenbild,* 67–71, indicates that Innocent completed the work in April, 1216, three months before his death.

11. Colin Morris, *The Papal Monarchy: the Western Church from 1050 to 1250* (Oxford: Clarendon, 1989), 418–19.

12. *Gesta,* PL 214: 5.

13. *Gesta,* PL 214: 17.

14. Helene Tillmann, *Pope Innocent III,* trans. Walter Sax (New York: North-Holland Publishing Co., 1980), 308 n. 51.

15. *Gesta,* PL 214: 187.

16. Sermon Two.

17. Mk. 16:16.

18. Acts 2:4.

19. James J. Murphy, *Rhetoric in the Middle Ages: A History of Rhetorical Theory from Saint Augustine to the Renaissance,* (Berkeley: University of California Press, 1974), 298–300.

20. For example, see the conversion of Clovis, *Gregory of Tours: The History of the Franks,* trans. Lewis Thorpe (Harmondsworth and Baltimore: Penguin, 1974), II, 31.

21. See Willibald, "Life of St. Boniface," in *Anglo-Saxon Missionaries in Germany,* trans. C. H. Talbot (London and New York: Sheed and Ward, 1954), 46; Bede, "Life of St. Cuthbert," *The Age of Bede,* trans. J. F. Webb, ed. D. H. Farmer (Harmondsworth and New York: Penguin, 1965; repr. ed. 1983), 59–60.

22. *Verbum Abbreviatum,* PL 205: 44.

23. Maurus, *De clericorum,* PL 107; Guibert, *Liber quo,* PL 156; trans. Joseph M. Miller, *Today's Speech,* vol. 17 (1969), 45–56.

24. Alan of Lille, *Summa,* PL 210: 189–91; *The Art of Preaching,* trans. Gillian R. Evans, (Kalamazoo, Michigan: Cistercian Publications, 1981).

25. Bernard Hamilton, "The Albigensian Crusade," in *Monastic Reform, Catharism and the Crusades, 900–1300* (1974; reprint, London: Variorum Reprints, 1979), VIII, 32.

26. For recent scholarship on the Cathars see Malcolm Lambert, *The Cathars (Peoples of Europe)* (Malden, MN: Blackwell Publishers, 1998); and R. I. Moore, *The Formation of a Persecuting Society: Power and Deviance in Western Europe, 950–1250* (Malden, MN: Blackwell Publishers, 1991).

27. Edward A. Synan, "The Pope's Other Sheep," in *The Religious Roles of the Papacy: Ideals and Realities, 1150–1300,* ed. Ryan, 402.

28. For thorough discussion of medieval sermon development see Murphy on *Ars praedicandi,* 269–355.

29. Frederick Imkamp, "Sermo Ultimus, quem facit Dominus Innocentius papa tercius in Lateranansi concilio generali," *Römische Quartalschrift* 70 (1975), 149–78.

30. Murphy, 325.

31. Hom. 5 *In Isaiam*, PG 56: 131.

32. *De mysteriis*, PL 217: 780A. For a general description of twelfth-century discussions of priesthood see Marcia L. Colish, *Peter Lombard*, vol. 2 (Leiden: E. J. Brill, 1994), 614–28.

33. Lev. 13 and 14; Lk. 17:12–14.

34. Sir. 45:21.

35. That this word takes its root from *pons*, "bridge," enforces the notion of the priest as nexus with divinity; see Albert Blaise, *Le vocabulaire latin des principaux thèmes liturgiques* (Turnhout: Brepols, 1966), s.v. *pontifex*.

36. Sermon Two.

37. See Imkamp, *Kirchenbild*, 59–60, for gradations in Innocent's usage of "brothers and sons."

38. Karl Rahner, *Bishops: Status and Function*, trans. Edward Quinn (Baltimore: Helicon Press, 1964), 46.

39. *De mysteriis*, PL 217: 777–78.

40. Michele Maccarrone, *Vicarius Christi: Storia del Titolo Papale* (Rome: Facultas Theologica Pontificii Athenaei Lateranensis, 1952), 13, 109–18, cites the early use of the term "Vicar of Christ" for all clergy, Innocent and the curia introducing it as an exclusive papal title; Walter Ullmann, in *New Catholic Encyclopedia*, s.v. "Innocent III," locates Innocent's achievement as twofold, clarifying the "legal function of the Pope as the successor of St. Peter at the same time making precise the definition of Petrine powers as vicarious powers of Christ Himself." Robert L. Benson, "Plenitudo Potestatis: Evolution of a Formula from Gregory IV to Gratian," *Studia Gratiana* 11 (1967): 104–217, traces the expanding understandings of the term from the viewpoint of a legal historian successively from the Pseudo-Isidorean writers, to Gregory IV, to the eleventh-century reformers, and to its enshrinement in Gratian's legal work.

41. As well as Maccarrone, *Vicarius Christi*, we have found to be particularly helpful Friedrich Kempf, *Papsttum und Kaisertum bei Innocenz III* (Rome: Pontificia Universitas Gregoriana, 1954); all importantly James A. Watt, *The Theory of Papal Monarchy in the Thirteenth Century: the Contribution of the Canonists*, (New York: Fordham University Press, 1965), which also supplies a valuable bibliography of earlier scholarship; Brian Tierney, *Origins of Papal Infallibility 1150–1350: A Study on the Concepts of Infallibility, Sovereignty and Tradition in the Middle Ages*, (Leiden: E. J. Brill, 1972), for needed clarifications on papal indefectibility; Pennington, *Pope and Bishops: The Papal Monarchy in the Twelfth and Thirteenth Centuries* (University of Pennsylvania Press, 1984), a fine legal history of Innocent III; Imkamp, *Kirchenbild*, for theology; Karlfried Froehlich, "Saint Peter, Papal Primacy, and the Exegetical Tradition, 1150–1300," in *Religious Roles of the Papacy*, ed. Ryan, 4–44, for a concise and thorough account of Innocent's contribution to the scriptural basis for the claim of plenitude; finally Yves M.-J. Congar, "Homo spiritualis: Usage juridique et politique d'un terme d'anthropologie chrétienne," in *Aus Kirche und Reich: Studien zu Theologie, Politik und Recht im Mittelalter*, ed. Hubert Mordek (Sigmaringen: Jan Thorbecke Verlag, 1983), 1–10, who writes with great perception about the Pope's and bishops' unavoidable obligation to speak out against wrongs.

42. Morris, 432.

43. Bernhard Schimmelpfennig, *The Papacy*, trans. James Sievert (New York: Columbia University Press, 1992), 181. Yves M.-J. Congar, "Status Ecclesiae," *Studia Gratiana* 15 (1972): 3–31, has traced the history of the term *status Ecclesiae*, including the relationship between the Pope's responsibility of caring for the good order of church and society (*sollicitudo*) and his use of power (*plenitudo potestatis*) to foster that aim. In the context of Lateran IV the phrase sets up the Pope's effort at reform, i.e., bringing the actual, existential state of the church into conformity with its ideal state of health, stability, peace, common utility, good of the whole; see p. 18.

44. Froehlich, 6, who explains, 38 and *passim*, Leo I "was the first to use the triad of Matt. 16:18f., Luke 22:32, and John 21:15–17 as primatial texts." Further, p. 4, "the understanding of the Petrine texts by Biblical exegetes in the mainstream of the tradition was universally non-primatial before Innocent III, and that it was the innovative exegetical argumentation of this imposing Pope which began to change the picture."

45. "This does not mean that Innocent regarded himself as 'infallible' either as a person or as an office-holder. . . . Innocent was aware of the canonical possibility of an erring pope (c. 6 Dist. 40 *Decreti Gratiani*). Nevertheless, Jesus' prayer rendered such a case unlikely in his opinion." See Froehlich, 26 n. 74; 25. Also see Brian Tierney, "A Scriptural Text in the *Decretales* and in St. Thomas: Canonistic Exegesis of Luke 22:32," *Studia Gratiana* 20 (1976): 363–77, who makes the point that inerrancy was considered an attribute of the church. Innocent discusses the loss of faith by a pope in Sermon Four.

46. *Liber regulae pastoralis*, also known as *Pastoral Care*, trans. and annotated Henry Davis (Westminster, MD: Newman Press, 1950).

47. *De consideratione*, in *Sancti Bernardi Opera*, vol. 3, ed. Jean Leclercq and Henri Rochais (Rome, 1963) hereafter cited as *De consid.*, giving book, section, paragraph. For the translation of *rusticani sudoris* as "sweating peasant," see *Five Books on Consideration: Advice to a Pope*, trans. John D. Anderson and Elizabeth T. Kennan (Kalamazoo: Cistercian Publications, 1976), [2.6.9] 56.

48. Watt, *Theory of Papal Monarchy*, 40.

49. *On Royal and Papal Power*, trans. James A. Watt (Toronto: Pontifical Institute of Mediaeval Studies, 1971), 163.

50. *Regestum Innocentii III papae super negotio Romani imperii*, ed. Friedrich Kempf (Rome: Pontificia Universitas Gregoriana, 1948), 47; PL 216: 1013B, no. 18, NRI, The Pope to the Nuntios of Philip [of Swabia] in Consistory.

51. Yves M.-J. Congar, "Ecce constitui te super gentes et regna (Jer. 1:10) 'in Geschichte und Gegenwart,'" in *Theologie Geschichte und Gegenwart: Michael Schmaus zum sechzigten Geburtstag dargebracht von sein Freunden und Schülern*, ed. Johann Auer and Herman Volk (Munich: Karl Zink Verlag, 1957), 672.

52. Congar, "Homo spiritualis," 2.

53. Marcia L. Colish, *The Mirror of Language: A Study in the Medieval Theory of Knowledge* (Lincoln: University of Nebraska Press, 1968), xi.

54. J. P. Migne, ed., *Patrologiae Cursus Completus Series Latina*, 222 vols. (Turnholt: Brepols; repr. ed., 1958), hereafter cited as PL, vol. 217, which contains the most easily ac-

cessible collection of Innocent's sermons. The collection includes twenty-nine sermons for the liturgical seasons, thirty-one for feast days, and twelve for the Common
of Saints, in addition to seven *De diversis*, 649–88, one of which, Sermon Five, is not
Innocent's work. A recent informative overview of the sermons is provided in John C.
Moore, "The Sermons of Pope Innocent III," *Römische Historische Mitteilungen* 36 (1994):
82–142. Giuseppe Scuppa, *I Sermoni di Innocenzo III* (Rome: Dissertation, Pontificia
Universitas Lateranensis, 1961), 204–7, offers an additional sermon, *First Sermon on the
Consecration of a Pontiff*, which may be a sketch for another anniversary address. We have
not translated it here.

55. PL 217: 309–11 for the letter.

56. Scuppa, 93.

57. *Opera Innocentii pontificis maximi, eius nominis III* . . . (Coloniae: excudebat Ioannes
Nouesianus, 1552); *D. Innocentii pontificis maximi eius nominis III . . . opera . . .* (Coloniae:
apud M. Cholinum, 1575). Connie Mae Munk discusses the Cologne editions in the
"Preface" to her edition of Sermon Three in *A Study of Pope Innocent III's Treatise: "De
quadripartita specie nuptiarum,"* vol. 2 (University of Kansas, Dissertation; Ann Arbor,
Michigan: University Microfilms, 1975), ii; note that each of the two editions and two
translations begins with page 1. See also Scuppa, 64 and Imkamp, *Kirchenbild*, 64–65.

58. Alan of Lille, *Summa* , PL 210: 189.

59. Munk, vol. 2, 1–12.

60. Prologue, 51v–52r; Sermons, 132v–140r.

61. In PL the sermons are ordered and titled: One, "On the Consecration of the
Pontiff"; Two, "On the Consecration of the Supreme Pontiff"; Three, "On the Con-
secration of the Pontiff"; Four, "On the Consecration of the Pontiff"; Six, "Given at
the General Council of the Lateran"; Seven, "Given at the General Council of the
Lateran." In *BL Add.* the sermons appear in different order and with different titles:
"In Synod" (Migne's Seven), "In Council of Priests" (One); "On a Confessor"
(Two); no titles, or the rubric of Two extends to Three and Four. Six is absent.

62. Eyewitness accounts exist which testify that Sermon Six was delivered at the
pre-dawn Mass opening the Council, and that copies of it had been prepared ahead
of time for distribution immediately after the session; Stephan Kuttner and Antonio
García y García, "A New Eyewitness Account of the Fourth Lateran Council," *Traditio* 20 (1964): 123.

63. Scuppa, 106.

64. *The Anchor Bible with Introductions, Translations, and Notes* (Garden City, N.Y.: Doubleday, 1964– ) and *The New Jerusalem Bible*, ed. Henry Wansbrough et al. (Garden City,
N.Y.: Doubleday, 1985).

65. The *Glossa Ordinaria* is a scholastic commentary on, and analysis of, the Bible,
done by adding notes, written in small script, to the margins of the handwritten Biblical texts. Additional commentary, in even smaller script, was added in brief notes
between the lines of the text. For centuries the *Glossa* was a widely used resource for
exegesis.

66. *Biblia Latina cum glossa ordinaria: Facsimile reprint of the editio princeps of Adolph Busch of
Strassburg 1480/81*, Introduction by Karlfried Froehlich and Margaret T. Gibson, 4

vols. (Brepols: Turnhout, 1992), hereafter entitled *Glossa*, with volume and page numbers. We also quote from PL 113 and 114, Migne's truncated edition.

## Notes to Prologue

1. Scuppa, 93.

2. For an excellent history and explanation of *Ars dictaminis* see Murphy, 194–268.

3. *Register* 2, no. 141, PL 214: 695–98.

4. The ordination of priests included a specific conferring of the power to preach, an official sanction not available to unauthorized preachers.

5. *Leviticus 1–16: A New Translation with Introduction and Commentary*, The Anchor Bible (New York: Doubleday, 1991), 504.

6. This is discussed at length and in these same terms by Gregory, *Pastoral Care* 2.4, PL 77: 31, trans. Davis, 51–55; repeated for instance in Gratian D. 43 c. 1.

7. Moore, "Sermons of Pope Innocent III," 82

8. Raymonde Foreville, *Le Pape Innocent III et la France*, Päpste und Papsttum 26 (Stuttgart: Hiersemann, 1992), 230–37.

9. *The Ordinal of the Papal Court from Innocent III to Boniface VIII and Related Documents* (Fribourg: University Press, 1975), xxi.

10. Innocent first identifies his sacerdotal rank, "bishop," then his ecclesiastical position as Pope through the title *servus servorum Dei*, a designation used in papal correspondence since the pontificate of Gregory the Great (590–604). For views of the title during Innocent's tenure and for his ability to pun tellingly on the title, see Stephan Kuttner, "Universal Pope or Servant of God's Servants: The canonists, papal titles, and Innocent III," *Revue de droit canonique* 32 (1981): 109–23. *Salutem et apostolicam benedictionem*, the conventional greeting in papal letters, had been standardized by the tenth century; see Carol Dana Lanham, "Salutation Formulas in Latin Letters to 1200: Syntax, Style, and Theory," *Münchener Beiträge zur Mediavistik und Renaissance-Forschung* 22 (1975): 10 n. 24.

11. Is. 32:20.

12. Lk. 8:11.

13. Rev. 19:6.

14. Prov. 11:26 and Mt. 25:18.

15. Lk. 10:35. In *De mysteriis* 29, PL 217: 816–17, Innocent notes that the apostolic epistles of the New Testament are supererogations, or additions, to the gospels, since Greek *epistolē* is translated as Latin *superrogatio*. Thus Innocent sees in the parable of the good Samaritan that the Samaritan is Christ; the two denarii left on deposit are the Gospel; the innkeeper is the order of apostles and their successors, who are to carry on the work of their absent Lord and are specifically enjoined to labor beyond the two denarii; this they are to do by writing and preaching.

16. Mt. 25:14–30.

17. Ex. 28: 35.

18. 1 Cor. 1: 17.

19. 2 Tim. 4:2, 4:4.

20. Rom. 10:15, Is. 52:7, Nahum 1:15.

21. Is. 58:1.

22. Mt. 10:27. Alan of Lille, *Summa*, PL 210: 111–12, cites this passage to support part of his definition of preaching which he calls "public instruction in faith and behavior" *(morum et fidei instructio)*. Alan further explains that hidden teaching is suspect because heretics teach secretly so as to deceive.

23. Mk. 16:15.

24. Is. 40:4.

25. Balsam, with which chrism is made, is both a healing ointment and a perfume.

26. This sentence concludes with a paraphrase of a non-scriptural commission from the ordination ceremony.

27. Mt. 5:19.

28. Lk. 4:23.

29. *BL Add.: maledicte.*

30. Mt. 21:19; Mk. 11:13.

31. Mt. 13:52.

32. Dan. 13:52.

33. Song 1:10. The application of this passage to the rhetorical principle of audience adaptation is noted without attribution in both the marginal and the interlinear glosses in the *Glossa*, where the equation of gold to wisdom and silver to eloquence is quite clear. See the disquisition on this passage in *De quad.*, 964–65, glossing Ps. 44:14–15a; Connie Mae Munk edition 3.18, pp. 92–95.

34. Prov. 21:20. Song of Songs and Proverbs were ascribed to Solomon, whose name is associated with the gift of wisdom in 1 Kings 3:10.

35. Ps. 11:7.

36. *BL Add.: doctores.* Marvin H. Pope, *Song of Songs: A New Translation with Introduction and Commentary*, The Anchor Bible (Garden City, N.Y., Doubleday, 1977), 345, cites this medieval interpretation: "The neck, as the channel for the passage of food and of speech, was seen as representing the Doctors of the Church who communicate the doctrine of Christ to the people; they are the link between the Head, which is Christ, and His second body, which is the faithful laity."

37. In this context "perfect" means "mature," as contrasted with those who have not reached Christian adulthood.

38. 1 Cor. 2:6; 2:2; 3:1–2.

39. Lk. 8:10.

40. Jn. 16:12.

41. Mt. 7:6.

42. Lev. 11:3; Deut. 14:6. According to God's command, among the animals that are "clean" and can therefore be eaten are those with cloven hooves who also ruminate, or chew the cud. *Glossa*, PL 113: 464, reads the dietary laws as laws of the spiritual life: "The church receives and incorporates into its body those who have an ungulate hoof, that is, who are known to have discretion between good and evil, and who ruminate, that is, meditate on the law day and night" ("Illos recipit Ecclesia et mem-

bris suis incorporat, qui ungulam findunt, qui discretionem boni et mali habere sci-
unt, et qui ruminant, id est meditantur in lege die et nocte").

43. The wine and the oil represent medicinal care for the sick (Lk. 10:34), in this
case medicine for spiritual ailments, the wine to stimulate, the oil to soothe; the rod
and the manna represent the means of moving people forward toward good, the rod
being a punishment or goad (e.g., Ezek. 7:11) while the manna is a nourishing entice-
ment (Ex. 16:31–35); the fire and the water are both means of cleansing, the water by
usual means, the fire as a more radical purging of impurity. The water also represents
the sacrament of Baptism, and the fire is associated with the Holy Spirit (Acts 2:3),
and thus with the sacrament of Confirmation. This is a prescription for using both
correction and reward as means of persuasion.

44. Alan of Lille identifies the "formation of men" *(informatio hominum)* as the
purpose of preaching, and the "foundation" *(fundamentum)* of preaching as theological authority drawn from Scripture; see *Summa*, PL 210: 112 and 113.

45. Eccles. 4:12. The rope that is loosened, *dissolvatur*, has overtones from philoso-
phy and rhetoric, where *dissolvere* means "to refute" or "to reply to." Thus the threads
of a well-woven argument cannot be easily untied.

46. Mt. 10:14.

47. 1 Cor. 9:27.

48. *causarum*. While this plea that he is overburdened is a rhetorical commonplace,
Innocent's workload was indeed extremely heavy. Among the exigencies of his papal
office he had, for instance, reestablished the triweekly papal consistories. He is so burdened that he ruefully likens himself in *Register* 6, no. 193, PL 215: 220A, to Jacob's wife
Leah, who suffered from being bleary-eyed (Gen. 29:17).

49. *proposui et dictavi*. Scuppa, 79–80, has suggested that these words be reversed in
order. We concur. Scuppa also notes that the technical term *proponere* has the significance of "pronunciare, rivolgere un discorso," to deliver a speech, perhaps evidence
that Innocent had indeed preached the sermons publically.

50. The sermons as we know them are all recorded in Latin. As for delivery, *Gesta*,
PL 214: 18, says that Innocent preached "sometimes in the vulgar tongue and sometimes in the literary." It was the custom to preach to the clergy in Latin and to the
people in the vernacular.

## Notes to Sermon One

1. Gratian, D. 18 (Friedberg 1:53–58). The ecumenical councils, such as Lateran IV,
were empowered to define doctrine, write legislation, and institute specific reforms.

2. Raymonde Foreville, *Le Pape Innocent III et la France*, 168, highlights the need Innocent saw for this reform, particularly within the episcopate, both in the personal lives
of the clergy and in their exercise of priestly offices.

3. By our reading of Werner Maleczek, *Papst und Kardinalskolleg von 1191 bis 1216*,
377–92, the likelihood would have been greater before 1208 of there being cardinals in
his audience who were also at his election. John C. Moore, "Innocent III's *De Miseria*

*Humanae Conditionis: A Speculum Curiae?"* *Catholic Historical Review* 67 (1981): 563, argues that *De miseria* "accurately reflects the moral concerns of a conscientious curial statesman." He cites Maccarrone that *De miseria* depicts "the ambience of the Roman Curia in which Lothario lived" (555).

4. Ezek. 9:6.

5. Abraham Ibn Ezra, a noted eleventh-century Jewish exegete, says of Lev. 4:3, "Scripture now goes into details, beginning with the High Priest (i.e. the kohen who is anointed). *that brings the people to guilt:* he has promulgated something that was incorrect, and the entire nation sinned unintentionally; by sinning, the High Priest inculpates every person. This expression is used because it is the High Priest who carries the burden of the Torah. He must be preserved from sin, because he is personally consecrated to GOD." *The Commentary of Abraham ibn Ezra on the Pentateuch. Volume 3: Leviticus,* trans. Jay F. Schachter (Hoboken, NJ: Ktav Publishing House, 1986), 10. For the influence of the Jewish exegetes on the Parisian scholastics, particularly through the work of Andrew of St. Victor, see Beryl Smalley, *The Study of the Bible in the Middle Ages* (Notre Dame, IN: University of Notre Dame Press, 1964), 156–72. That Innocent was familiar with these Jewish studies seems to be indicated by his reference to the Hebrew usage in the final paragraph of this sermon.

6. For a detailed summary of the arguments see Marcia L. Colish, *Peter Lombard* 2: 583–609 and Oscar D. Watkins, *A History of Penance: Being a Study of the Authorities,* vol. 2 (London: Longmans, Green, 1920), 726–49.

7. The act of anointing with special oils is used in many cultures as a means of consecrating or otherwise setting apart certain objects or persons as being sacred in some way. In the Hebrew and Christian traditions it is a usual part of conferring priesthood and often royalty (Ex. 29:29; 1 Sam. 15:17).

8. Lev. 4:3.

9. *BL Add.: synagogus.* Particularly helpful for this sermon is the discussion of these four "socio-religious" categories of persons by Jacob Milgrom, *Leviticus 1–16,* 226–32.

10. Juvenal, *Satires* 8.140–41. Translation ours. Cf. *Juvenal and Persius,* trans. G. G. Ramsay, Loeb Classical Library (Cambridge, MA: Harvard University Press, 1940), 168.

11. Sir. 12:13.

12. Lk. 12:49.

13. Wis. 6:6.

14. Lk. 8:10.

15. Lk. 12:47.

16. Mt. 16:19.

17. Ezek. 13:19.

18. 1 Cor. 11:29.

19. Rom. 2:24.

20. Jn. 5:19.

21. Mt. 10:25.

22. Cf. Rom. 2:21–22.

23. Gratian, C. 11 q. 3 c. 3 (Friedberg 1: 643), quoting Gregory, *Pastoral Care* 3.4,

trans. Davis, 97: the priest's sin not only condemns the priest, but also makes him responsible for the ruin of those in his care.

24. Is. 1:5–6.

25. Henry Davis in Gregory, *Pastoral Care*, 258 n. 173: "Very strangely, this apothegm, repeatedly quoted by the Fathers as in the Bible, is not found there. It is adduced as Biblical in the *Didache* and by St. Augustine, *Ennar[rationes] in Ps[almos]* 102.12."

26. Jn. 8:34.

27. Ps. 49:16.

28. *De mysteriis*, PL 217: 780A.

29. Lk. 4:23.

30. Lk. 6:42.

31. Is. 6:6–7.

32. Mal. 2:2.

33. Is. 1:15.

34. Lev. 5:2.

35. Mt. 5:16.

36. Ps. 50:19.

37. Mt. 11:30.

38. Ps. 50:21.

39. Literally, "by confession of his mouth," an awkward phrase in English.

40. The raising from the dead of Jairus's young daughter (Mt. 9:25), of the widow's adolescent son (Lk. 7:12–15), and of Lazarus (Jn. 11:44). Innocent employs this figure quite allusively here, though he develops it in copious detail in Sermon 10 *De sanctis*, PL 217: 493C–496C.

41. 2 Cor. 5:6.

42. Ps. 140:3.

43. Is. 43:9.

44. Prov. 18:17.

45. *BL Add: accusat* and *In septem psalmos*, PL 217: 1017B, 1060B.

46. Lk. 18:9–18. PL gives "etc." here. Innocent may have repeated the whole lengthy parable, or, with this cue, assumed his listeners would make the necessary inferences about it.

47. *In septem psalmos*, PL 217: 1017B; see also Alan of Lille, *Summa*, PL 210: 172.

48. Ps. 68:16.

49. Lk. 9:58. Alan of Lille, *In distinctionibus dictionum theologicalium*, PL 210: 1011A, gives "Men are called deceitful, who are delighted by their [own] deceits, which they hide in their hearts, as in the Gospel, 'The foxes have holes.'"

50. Hos. 14:3.

51. *In septem psalmos*, PL 217: 1060C.

52. Rev. 2:23.

53. Heb. 4:13.

54. Ezek. 18:22. *In septem psalmos*, PL 217: 1017C.

55. Mt. 6:17.

56. Ps. 118:109.

57. Rom. 12:1: Lk. 3:8.

58. Ps. 34:13.

59. Ps.118: 62.

60. Alan of Lille, *Summa*, PL 210: 121, identifies the "beast," *jumentum*, as the "flesh," *caro*, that may become "wanton," *lasciviat*, for lack of penance.

61. Rom. 6:19.

62. Mt. 23:4.

63. 1 Pet. 2:24.

64. Deut. 32:39.

65. Alan of Lille, *Summa*, PL 210: 171–72, credits Isidore with this statement.

66. 2 Pet. 2:22.

67. Jn. 5:9.

68. Mk. 16:9.

69. Lk. 8:30–33.

70. Cf. Mt. 12:43–45; Lk. 11:24–26.

71. Innocent had first read the clause "who is anointed" as set off with commas, i.e., as synonymous with *priest;* here he presents it without commas, i.e., as non-synonymous with *priest*, as in Lev. 21:17–23. Aaron's male descendants were to be anointed in the priesthood, except those with physical impediments, who were assigned other services to fulfill. This requirement of being flawless extended into the moral realm, as in Prov. 9 and Job 11:14–15.


## Notes to Sermon Two

1. *Gesta*, PL 214: 20. Tradition maintains that St. Peter was the first Bishop of Antioch, before becoming Bishop of Rome. The chair (*cathedra* or *sedes*) was the seat from which bishops, including St. Peter, presided, and as such it became a symbol of episcopal jurisdiction, hence the bishop's "see" (seat) and "Chair of St. Peter." The term *apostolic seat*, indicating the Bishop of Rome in the exercise of his episcopal office as the successor of Peter, pertains to the office, not to a material chair; see Michele Maccarrone, "The 'Chair of St. Peter' in the Middle Ages: from Symbol to Relic," in *Romana Ecclesia Cathedra Petri*, ed. Piero Zerbi et al. (Rome: Herder, 1991), 1279. In Innocent's day there was venerated in Rome a wooden chair thought to have been the genuine chair of St. Peter, but which was probably one donated to the papacy by Charles the Bald in 875. Innocent III used the wooden seat for the ceremonies that day, and found it felicitous that he was being consecrated on the Feast of the Chair. Today, a wooden chair, likely the same one, is encased within a bronze chair in the tribune of St. Peter's; see Michele Maccarrone et al., "Memorie," in *Atti Della Pontifica Accademia Romana Archeologia*, Serie III (Tipografia Poliglotta Vaticana, 1971), 21.

2. Bernard Jacqueline, pointing out St. Bernard's influence upon Sermon Two, goes so far as to call Innocent III Bernard's disciple, in *Episcopat et papauté chez saint Bernard de Clairvaux* (Saint-Lo: Editions Henri Jacqueline, 1975), 304. He also points

out, p. 20, the influence of Gregory on Bernard's work, including the usage of the title word *consideration*, "a monastic term for contemplation found in the *Liber regulae Pastoralis*."

3. Jer. 1:10. See Introduction 20–23 for Innocent's application of this verse.

4. Bernard, *De consid*. 2.6.9, ed. Leclercq and Rochais, 417: "Disce sarculo tibi opus esse, non sceptro, ut opus facias Prophetae. Et quidem ille non regnaturus ascendit, sed exstirpaturus." Trans. Anderson and Kennan, 56.

5. Ibid. 3.5.19, ed. Leclercq and Rochais, 446: "aut neglectu incultum, aut fraude subreptum." Trans. Anderson and Kennan, 104.

6. Ibid. 2.6.9, ed. Leclercq and Rochais, 416: "impositum . . . ministerium, non dominium datum." Trans. Anderson and Kennan, 56.

7. Ibid. 3.1.2, ed. Leclercq and Rochais, 432: "Ita et tu praesis ut provideas, ut consulas, ut procures, ut serves." Trans. Anderson and Kennan, 80.

8. *Gesta*, PL 214: 20–21.

9. Mt. 24:45.

10. "Veritas" is a feminine noun that here refers to Christ. For that reason we have translated the "ipsa" as "himself" rather than as "herself" or "itself."

11. Rev. 19:16.

12. Ex. 15:3; Ps. 67:5; Jer. 33:2; Amos 5:8, 9:6.

13. Mt. 16:18.

14. 1 Cor. 3:10–11.

15. Mt. 8:24–27. Peter's storm-tossed boat is a well-used figure of the existential difficulties of the church; Hugo Rahner, "Zur Symbolgeschicte des römischen Primats," *Zeitschrift für katholische Theologie* 69 (1947): 1–35; Wilhelm Imkamp, *Kirchenbild*, 274–77. The figure has a contextual immediacy, for it opens the Election Decree of 1059, which would almost certainly have been reviewed by the Cardinal Electors at the time of Innocent's election, six weeks before. Note the effective double meaning of the clause, "especially when Jesus sleeps in it": the boat *will not be submerged* because *Jesus* sleeps in it; also, the boat *is tossed* because Jesus *sleeps* in it. "Jesus asleep" signified troubled times, as in Cecily Clark, ed., *The Peterborough Chronicle*, rev. ed. (Oxford: Clarendon Press, 1970), 56, the year 1137.

16. *Glossa* 4: 75.

17. Mt. 7:25.

18. 1 Cor. 10:4.

19. Ps. 4:2.

20. Mt. 28:20.

21. Rom. 8:31.

22. The wolf represents false prophets (Jn. 10:12). *Lupus* may be a a substitution for *vulpes*, the foxes, representing false teachers, who destroy the vines (Song 2:15). Innocent names both animals as figures of heretics who threaten the bishops' care for their flocks: e.g., *lupus* in *Register* 1 no. 160, PL 214, 135; *vulpes* in *Register* 2 no. 63, PL 214: 602ff. The "perfidious wolves" are also mentioned in the ordination ceremony as abductors of the sheep. The references made in this catena are used frequently to describe the church: the vine is Christ, and his apostles are the branches (Jn. 15:5); the tu-

nic is Christ's seamless garment, for which the Roman soldiers gambled during the crucifixion (Jn. 19:23–24); the light on the candlestick represents the good works which glorify God (Mt. 5:15–16).

23. Acts 5:38–39.

24. Ps. 117:6.

25. As in *servus servorum Dei*, a jurisdictional term employed by Innocent from the time of his election, when he took over the administration of the church. See Prologue n.10.

26. Jn. 8:34.

27. Mt. 18:32.

28. Lk. 12:47.

29. Lk. 17:10.

30. Vulgate *benefici*, "benefactors:" PL *venefici*, "poisoners."

31. Lk. 22:25–26. This definition is in agreement with the traditional understanding of the prelate's role. Gregory the Great, *Pastoral Care* 2.6, trans. Davis, 65, had quoted this passage from Luke to emphasize the importance of subduing the lust for power, and Bernard of Clairvaux had admonished the Pope that it is not becoming for him to lord it over those who have been generous to him, but rather he should be generous, i.e., beneficent, to them; *De consid.* 3.3.13, ed. Leclercq and Rochais, 439–40; trans. Anderson and Kennan, 93.

32. This contrast of ministry with dominion echoes Bernard, *De consid.* 2.6.9, ed. Leclercq and Rochais, 416; trans. Anderson and Kennan, 56. Cf. note 6 above. A *ministerium* in its first meaning is domestic service, probably of the sort referred to in the Gospel passage from which the sermon is drawn. By extension it has come to mean the office of court official, public office holder, judge, pastor, or administrator of the sacraments. The common characteristic of these roles is service, the meaning that it carries throughout the sermon. *Dominium*, in contrast, means sovereignty or rulership, which is the role of the master, in this case Christ. This point is explained by Innocent in Sermon 1 *De communes*, PL 217: 599.

33. 1 Pet. 5:3.

34. 2 Cor. 11:23.

35. Wilhelm Imkamp, "'Pastor et sponsus': Elemente einer Theologie des bischöflichen Amtes bei Innocenz III," in *Aus Kirche und Reich: Studien zu Theologie, Politik und Recht im Mittelalter*, Festschrift für Friedrich Kempf, ed. Hubert Mordek (Jan Thorbecke Verlag: Sigmaringen, 1983), 287 n. 16, cites Innocent's word play taken from chime words: "nomen episcopi plus sonat *oneris* quam *honoris*." Innocent is fond of the figure, e.g. *De mysteriis*, PL 217: 777–78; *Register 2*, no. 4 and 60, PL 214: 542 and 596. Augustine in *De civitate Dei*, PL 41: 647, had defined episcopacy as "the title of a work, not of an honor." The figure was current. Alan of Lille, *Summa*, PL 210: 183D–184, similarly chides dilatory prelates who want the honors of their clerical status, yet are too lazy to preach.

36. Rom. 1:14. Latin *debitum*, "debt," also "duty." In *De consid.* 3.1.2, ed. Leclercq and Rochais, 432–33, Bernard comments that the "bothersome name of debtor better suits a servant than a ruler. . . . you are a debtor to the infidel, whether Jew, Greek, or

Gentile" (Latin: "debitoris molestum nomen servienti potius quam dominanti con-gruere. . . . Ergo et infidelibus debitor es, Iudaeis, Graecis, et Gentibus"). Trans. An-derson and Kennan, 80.

37. 2 Cor. 11:28–29.

38. Ps. 18:3.

39. Job 6:12.

40. 2 Cor. 3:5.

41. Jas. 1:5.

42. Jer. 10:23.

43. Mt. 14:29–31.

44. Is. 40:4; Lk 3:5.

45. Innocent amplifies the "contract" trope introduced at the opening of the ser-mon and stresses it as a legal agreement. *Condicio* in a legal contract "makes the validi-ty thereof dependent upon the occurrence or non-occurrence of a future event"; and *debitum* is "the obligatory tie between debtor and creditor"; Berger s.v.

46. Innocent's faithfulness is double. Within the "contract," he is to maintain not only an "honest keeping of one's promises and performing the duties assumed by agreement," but also "the confidence, trust, faith one has in another's behavior, partic-ularly with regard to the fulfillment of his liabilities." He will be faithful to Christ, and he will have very great faith that Christ will fulfill his part of the contract. See Berger, s.v. *fides*.

47. Rom. 10:10. The confession indicated here is oral profession of the faith rather than oral confession of sins. Innocent distinguishes, *In septem psalmos*, PL 217: 1015B: "There is the confession of the sinner, the confession of the praiser, and the confes-sion of the advocate" ("Est confessio peccatoris, confessio laudatoris, et confessio as-sertoris.").

48. Gen. 15:6. Cf. Rom. 4:3.

49. Heb. 11:6.

50. Rom. 14:23.

51. Lk. 22:32.

52. Heb. 5:7, discussing Christ's role as High Priest.

53. *Privilegium*, "A legal enactment concerning a specific person or case and involv-ing an exemption from common rules." Berger, s.v. *privilegium*, in this case a law which applies only to Peter and his successors.

54. Jn. 3:18. That the Pope can be judged by men as to the orthodoxy of his faith is a major topic of Sermon Four.

55. *catholice*, literally, "catholicly."

56. Lk. 8:48 and Jn. 8:11.

57. Jas. 2:20.

58. Hab. 2:4 and Heb. 10:38.

59. Rom. 2:13.

60. Jas. 1:23–24:

61. Mt. 10:16.

62. Rom. 12:1.

63. Mt. 6:3.

64. Deut. 17:8.

65. Is. 5:20. In the ordination ceremony of priest and bishops the duty of discernment is linked specifically to the "faithful and prudent servant."

66. Ezek. 13:19.

67. For a description of the *logion*, also called *ephod* and *rationale*, see Ex. 28.

68. Mt. 15:14.

69. 2 Cor. 3:6.

70. *ad omnem prudentiam;* R.E. Latham, *Revised Medieval Latin Word List from British and Irish Sources* (London, The British Academy: Oxford Univ. Press, 1973), s.v. *prudentia*, (pl.) "learned authorities." *Auctoritates* includes Biblical and patristic texts, as well as legal commentators and decisions of lower courts.

71. Sir. 31:9.

72. Bernard, *De consid.* 2.5.8, ed. Leclercq and Rochais, 416; trans. Anderson and Kennan, 56.

73. Jer. 1:10.

74. Mt. 16:19.

75. Jn. 20:23. Innocent makes the distinction between *particulariter*, the limited powers given to bishops as successors of the Apostles, and *universaliter* or *generaliter*, the universal power given to the Pope as successor to Peter. See n. 53 above concerning Peter's "privilege." Kenneth Pennington, *Pope and Bishops*, 49, has shown that Innocent is an "inventive and original exegete" in quoting this particular Scripture to support his point that the "mandate to Peter had not included the other apostles."

76. Mt. 16:19.

77. Jn. 1:42.

78. Aramaic *kepha (kepa)* means "rock;" and Latin *petra*, a cognomen for the apostle Peter. The mistaken association of those terms with the Greek *cephas (cephale)*, Latin *caput*, "head," was common for centuries, although the words have no etymological connection. For a full discussion of the usage see Yves M.-J. Congar, "Cephas-Céphalè-Caput," *Revue du moyen âge latin* 8 (1952): 5–42.

79. Ex. 7:1. God appointed Moses to a position of power over the Pharaoh of Egypt that was analogous to that of God's. See Helene Tillmann, *Pope Innocent III*, 40 n. 4, for further background on the interpretation of "god of Pharoah."

80. 1 Cor. 4:4.

81. 1 Pet. 5:5, and James 4:6.

82. Lk. 14:11.

83. Is. 40:4.

84. Sir. 3:20.

85. Sir. 32:1.

86. Sir. 26:17 and Mt. 5:15–16. The sense of the argument here suggests that Innocent is gesturing toward himself as the *Haec*, "This." See n. 101 below.

87. Mt. 6:23.

88. Mt. 5:13. Sermon Four is Innocent's explication of this text.

89. Lk. 12:48.

90. Jn. 10:16.
91. Song 6:8.
92. See n. 22 above.
93. Cf. Gen. 6–7.
94. Mt. 16:18–19.
95. Lk. 22:31–32.
96. Jn. 21:15–17.
97. *Glossa* 4:76.
98. Jn. 4:34.
99. Sir. 15:3.
100. Jn. 6:56.
101. Mt. 5:16.
102. Mt. 5:15.
103. Lk. 12:35. This description of the servant on watch will recur in Sermon Six.
104. Lev. 4:3. Sermon One is Innocent's explication of this text.
105. Juvenal, *Satires* 8.140–41. Translation ours. Cf. Loeb edition, 168.
106. Mt. 25:14–30.
107. 1 Cor. 1:17.
108. Mt. 15:27.
109. Mt. 4:4, and Deut. 8:3.
110. Lam. 4:4.
111. Jn. 6:51–52, 54.
112. Eccles. 3:11.
113. Acts 1:1.
114. 1 Pet. 2:21–22 and Is. 53:9.
115. Mt. 5:19.
116. Ex. 28:34–35.
117. Lk. 4:23.
118. Mt. 7:5.
119. Rom. 2:21–22.
120. Ps. 49:16.
121. 1 Cor. 9:22.
122. Rom. 12:15.
123. Rom. 12:1.
124. 1 Cor. 2:6.
125. 1 Cor. 2:2.
126. 1 Cor. 3:1–2.
127. Heb. 5:14.
128. 1 Cor. 11:29.
129. 1 Tim. 2:8.

## Notes to Sermon Three

1. *Codice Barberini Latino 2733*, ed. Reto Niggl (Rome: Biblioteca Apostolica Vaticana, 1972), fig. 84, 158v–159r. Iconographically, each of Innocent's "four kinds of marriage" can be found represented therein.

2. *Register* 1, no. 530 (532) in Othmar Hageneder and Anton Haidacher, *Die Register Innocenz' III. Pontifikatsjahr, 1198/99* (Graz-Köln: Verlag Hermann Böhlaus, 1964), 765–69. Also from *Register* 1 see numbers 50, 51, 117, 335 (the famous *Quanto personam* concerning Conrad of Hildesheim; see Pennington, *Pope and Bishops*, 31–33), 447, 490, 502, 503.

3. Kenneth Pennington, review of Imkamp, *Kirchenbild*, in *Zeitschrift der Savigny-Stiftung für Rechtsgeschichte* 72 (1986): 425.

4. PL 217: 921–68.

5. This model was given a rationale by the Pseudo-Isidorean documents (c. 850) to defend "the rights of bishops against their metropolitans and, to a lesser extent, to claim early authority for Papal supremacy"; see *Oxford Dictionary of the Christian Church*, 2nd ed. (Oxford University Press, 1974), s.v. "False Decretals." Huguccio later taught that the election of a prelate, paralleling the marriage ceremony, creates an immediate and permanent bond: "Through the 'mutual consent' *(mutuus consensus)* of electors and electus, a 'spiritual marriage' *(matrimonium spirituale)* is contracted between them." See Robert Benson, *Bishop-Elect*, 122. See also Jean Gaudemet, "Le symbolisme du mariage entre l'évêque et son église et ses conséquences juridiques," in *Droit de l'église et vie sociale au moyen âge* (Northampton, Vermont: Variorum Reprints, 1989 [reprint of 1985]), 110–23.

6. Commentators found the triad a useful teaching device, long-honored in Augustine's "offspring, chastity, and sacrament;" see *De peccato originali*, PL 44: 406 and *De nuptiis et concupiscentia*, PL 44: 424. Innocent consistently uses *sacramentum* to mean indissolubility, a "sacred binding oath." See Berger, s.v. *sacra, sacramentum*.

7. Marcia L. Colish, *Peter Lombard* 1: 628–98, explains that there were two twelfth-century views of marriage: the effective moment was either consummation (Gratian) or consent (French schools). Innocent insists on consent, saying in this sermon that "consent alone effects marriage." For Gratian's discussion of these terms see C. 27 q. 34–C. 30 q. 5 (Friedberg 1: 1073–1108). See Seamus P. Heaney, *The Development of the Sacramentality of Marriage from Anselm of Laon to Thomas Aquinas* (Washington: The Catholic University of America Press, 1963), 15.

8. Benson, *Pope-Elect*, 160–61.

9. Papal Election Decree of Nicholas II (D. 23 c.1 Friedberg 1:77–79). Detlev Jasper newly edits and discusses the true and forged texts of the decree, *Das Papstwahldekret von 1059: Überlieferung und Textgestalt* (Sigmaringen: J. Thorbecke, 1986). A later decree in 1179 made it clear that two-thirds majority constitutes an election and thus invests the Pope immediately with the administrative prerogatives of his office irrespective of his consecration as bishop. Lateran Council III, by means of a constitutional innovation, put it beyond doubt that two-thirds of the votes "elected" the Pope and that "in the Roman church there is a special constitution, since no recourse

can be had to a superior." See Norman P. Tanner, *Decrees of the Ecumenical Councils*, 1: 205–11.

10. A helpful introduction to the subject is Jean Leclercq, *Monks on Marriage: A Twelfth Century View* (New York: The Seabury Press, 1983).

11. Pennington, *Pope and Bishops*, 123.

12. For reference see note 1 above. The Latin inscription reads as follows: "Summa Petri sedes est, haec sacra principis aedes / Mater cunctarum decor et decus ecclesiarum / Devotus Christi, qui templo servit in isto. / Flores virtutis capiet fructusque salutis."

13. Jn. 3:29.

14. John the Baptist is *paranymphus*, literally "bridesman," the best man. For metaphors of "voice" and of "lamp" see Lk. 3:4 and Mt. 5:35.

15. Cf. *Glossa*, PL 113: 1128A (on Song of Songs): "The groom, understand, is Christ; the bride is the church without stain or wrinkle" (Latin: "Sponsum, Christum intellige, sponsam Ecclesiam sine macula et ruga.").

16. Ps 18:6. Christ is the "sun of justice" (Mal. 4:2).

17. Song 4:9.

18. *De quad.* (PL 217: 921–68), from which Innocent quotes verbatim.

19. Gen. 2:24, quoted in Mark 10:7, Mt. 19:7, Eph. 5:31.

20. Rev. 21:9.

21. Hos. 2:19.

22. Song 3:11. *Solomon* and *shalom* share the root meaning of "peace," as the comment on the same quotation in *De quad.*, PL 217: 923B, explains: "O daughters of Sion . . . see . . . King *Solomon* (Song 3:11), that is, 'Christ the true *peace*maker who made one from two'" (Eph. 2:14), which in Latin reads, "O filiae Sion, . . . videte . . . Regem Salomonem, id est 'Christum verum pacificum, qui fecit utraque unum.'"

23. Gen. 2:24.

24. Mt. 19:6.

25. 1 Cor. 12:12. Wilhelm Imkamp, *Kirchenbild*, 182–96, gives a developed account and bibliography of the metaphor of the "body" in Innocent's theology; he relates it to the universal church, to the particular church, and to the individual, a matrix of networks similar to those Innocent lays out.

26. 1 Cor. 12:13.

27. 1 Cor. 6:17.

28. 1 Jn. 4:16.

29. Athanasian Creed (=Symbolum "Quicumque") of c. 381–428, H. Denzinger, *The Sources of Catholic Dogma*, trans. Roy J. Deferrari from the Thirtieth Edition of Henry Denzinger's *Enchiridion Symbolorum* (St. Louis: Herder, 1957), 15–16. A major portion of the creed expounds the doctrine that Jesus Christ has two natures, one divine and one human, united in a single Person.

30. Jn. 1:14.

31. As Imkamp stresses, *Kirchenbild*, 304, for Innocent and the tradition within which he writes, the marriages of man and woman, Christ and church, bishop and local diocese are not simple transpositions of one to the other: the first and exclusive

term they share is "indissolubility." Thus Innocent refers not to the sacrament of marriage as such, but to one of its "goods," which he will discuss.

32. Lk. 14:10, a nuptial banquet parable.

33. Jn. 21:17.

34. PL: *bona; BL Add.: dona.*

35. 2 Cor. 12:1.

36. Lk. 12:48.

37. Mt. 16:19.

38. Jer. 1:10.

39. Wis. 6:6.

40. Sir. 3:20.

41. Sir. 32:1.

42. Lk. 22:26.

43. Mt. 28:20.

44. Lk. 22:31–32.

45. 1 Jn. 5:4.

46. Heb. 5:7.

47. Ps. 117:6.

48. *BL Add.: sponsam.*

49. As Imkamp observes, *Kirchenbild*, 315, the phrase *Mater et Magistra* translates "marriage" of church/Christ into that of church/Bishop of Rome; through Baptism and Eucharist "procreation and rearing spiritual children, i.e. the care of souls, is made the urgent task" of the Pope.

50. Prov. 31:29. The names of these Old Testament heroines have become synonymous with certain of their traits: Sarah's maturity, because she was past childbearing age when she bore Isaac (Gen. 21:1–3); Rebecca's prudence in obtaining Isaac's blessing for Jacob, her favorite son, rather than having it go to Esau, the elder son, to whom it rightfully belonged (Gen. 27); Leah's fecundity, because she bore seven children to Jacob (Gen. 29:31–35 and Gen. 30:17–22); Rachel, the wife Jacob truly loved (Gen. 29:17–20); Hanna, who dedicated her son, Samuel, to God, even before his conception (1 Sam. 1:11–12); Susanna, who was saved by the prophet Daniel when falsely accused of being unchaste (Dan. 13); Judith, to whom God gave the courage to kill Holofernes, the Assyrian general, and so save her people from destruction by his army (Judith 13–15); and Esther, whose beauty saved the Hebrews from persecution under King Ahasuerus (Esther 5, 6, 7).

51. Here again "sacramental" refers to the indissolubility of the marriage contract, not to the sacrament of Marriage itself. See nn. 6 and 31 above.

52. Innocent adapts C. 32 q. 4. c. 6 (Friedberg 1:1129).

53. *manipulos*, sheaves. See Ps. 125:6.

54. Benson, *Bishop Elect*, 160, notes that Innocent draws from *Summa omnis qui iuste iudicat* (1180s) the "terse formulation which was repeated by later canonists from Huguccio to Hostiensis, 'By being elected, he is confirmed, and in being confirmed, he is elected.'"

55. D. 23 c.1 (Friedberg 1:77–79). Election did not, however, confer the spiritual powers that come with sacramental ordination.

56. As a hagiographic detail with perhaps some basis in fact, *Gesta* c. 6, PL 214: 20, reports that Innocent had sometimes dreamed he had married his mother.

57. C. 35 q. 2–3 c.16 (Friedberg 1:1268). *Propinqui* includes marriage among blood kindred, *consanguini*, and among in-laws, *affines*. See Berger s.v. *adfinitas, nuptiae incestuosae*, and Gratian C. 35 q. 1. Edward A. Synan, "The Pope's 'Other Sheep,'" in *Religious Roles of the Papacy*, 394, sees spiritual kinship being established through baptism. Innocent also implies a jurisdictional matrix: strangers (non-kin) are those from a different church, i.e. diocese.

58. Text amended according to D. 61 c. 13 (Friedberg 1: 231), which bespeaks the expectation that bishops will not be strangers, but may in fact be so.

59. Amending Migne's garbled text in line with D. 79 c. 3 (Friedberg 1:277), which specifies that only a cardinal, i.e., one already in the "family" of the Roman See, might be consecrated Pope. Innocent, a cardinal deacon at the time of his election, January 8, 1198, was ordained to the priesthood on Saturday, February 21, and consecrated bishop Sunday, February 22, 1198; *Gesta* c. 7, PL 214: 20. Stephan Kuttner, "Cardinalis: The History of a Canonical Concept," *Traditio* 3 (1943): 149–50, argues for seeing "cardinal" as one of the family. Kenneth Pennington, "Innocent III's Knowledge of Law," 12–14, discusses how Innocent's views differed from contemporary canonists about choosing a pope outside the cardinalate.

60. February 22, the Feast of Peter's Chair at Antioch. While the consecration itself would have occurred within the liturgy of February 22, an anniversary would not have precedence over so important a feast as "Peter's Chair." Connie Mae Munk, 1:178, cites one manuscript saying that the anniversary preceded February 22.

61. The importance Innocent attaches to his consecration as bishop, rather than Pope, is discussed by Wilhelm Imkamp, "Pastor et sponsus," 285–94.

62. *De quad.*, PL 217: 932A.

63. Jn. 10:14. As well as his efforts to restore heretics to the church, Innocent within ten months of election wrote Emperor Alexius III and Patriarch Georgias of Constantinople, considered schismatics, in an effort toward reconciliation; see *Register* 1, no. 353 and 354. The flock/family are those joined through Baptism, common faith, and community. Innocent, and some of his successors, also counted the Moslems and Mongols among their "other sheep," and wanted to add them to their progeny; Synan, "The Popes' 'Other Sheep,'" 398.

64. Jn. 10:5.

65. 1 Cor. 7:4.

66. Rom. 1:14.

67. 2 Cor. 11:28.

68. *BL Add.*: *possit*.

69. Gen. 16. "According to Mesopotamian law a barren wife could present one of her female slaves to the husband and acknowledge the issue as her own." *New Jerusalem Bible*, Gen. 16 note b.

70. Jn. 6:64.

71. Ostia and Velletri, two of the ancient, original seven suburban sees, had been united as recently as 1150. Innocent's example is apropos, because the Cardinal-bishop of Ostia and Velletri oversaw papal liturgies; to him fell the honor of consecrating the new Pope. Octavian, holder of the office at this time, was probably present for this Sermon, thus showing that there was no "need to look very far."

72. *Gratian*, C. 7 q. 1 c. 12 (Friedberg 1:571). In the fourth century, Valerius, the bishop of Hippo, fearing that Augustine might be made a bishop elsewhere, requested permission from the primate of Africa to have Augustine consecrated in Hippo as co-adjutor, with right of succession to the see. This was done, and when Valerius died in 396, Augustine became Bishop of Hippo. See *New Catholic Encyclopedia*, sub "St. Augustine."

73. *Quaestio*, a term of formal debate, is the technique of drawing opponents into making contradictory statements. Innocent has used *quaestiones* to frame his discussion (e.g., Am I not the bridegroom?).

74. *BL Add.: regeneret.*

75. Ps. 127:3.

76. Gal. 4:19.

77. See Gen. 30:14–18, and note "a," *New Jerusalem Bible:* mandrakes "were understood to be an aphrodisiac and fertility potion." Leah is figured as the Mother of Israel and of the Synagogue, a point more explicit in *De quad.,* PL 217: 932–33. Innocent will praise Leah in *Nisi cum pridum* (1206) "a eulogy of the episcopal office," as a model of pontifical efficacy, along with the Gospel example of Martha (Lk. 11:38–42), equating Martha's active life with Leah's fruitful one; see Pennington, *Pope and Bishops* 107–8.

78. *BL Add.: regenerat.*

79. Sir. 15:3.

80. Prov. 9:5.

81. Jn. 6:52.

82. Wis. 16:20.

83. Rom. 7:2.

84. *BL Add.* inserts *non transfertur,* Munk, 12.

85. Rom. 14:4; 1 Cor. 4:4. This idea is a major topic of Sermon Four.

86. Jn. 3:18.

87. Mt. 5:13. Pericope of Sermon Four.

88. *BL Add.: specialiter.*

89. Lk. 22:32.

90. Here Innocent follows his usual practice of juxtaposing *plenitudo potestatis* with *pars sollicitudinis.* See Introduction pp. 16–20.

91. The Pope received the mitre and the crown separately. The crown symbolized the secular authority of the Pope." Ian Stuart Robinson, *The Papacy, 1073–1198: Continuity and Innovation* (Cambridge: Cambridge University Press, 1990), 20. Robinson notes that the Pope was required to wear his crown on certain feast days. Among

those occasions was the Feast of St. Martin, the day on which Lateran Council IV was convened.

92. Rev. 19:16.

93. Ps. 109:4. Melchisedech, an enigmatic figure from the book of Genesis, was the king of Salem (peace) and a "Priest of the Most High" (Gen. 14:18), a contemporary of Abraham. In Psalm 109 he is presented as a figure of the Messiah; Gerald Thomas Kennedy, *St. Paul's Conception of the Priesthood of Melchisedech: An Historico-Exegetical Investigation* (Washington, D.C.: The Catholic University of America Press, 1951), 49–59. Not only is Melchisedech a person without genealogy—an unusual feature for a scriptural personality—but he also offered an unbloody sacrifice of bread and wine, the elements from which the Eucharist is confected in the Mass. In Heb. 6:20 it is the priesthood of Melchisedech, pre-existing that of Aaron, that is the priestly "Order" of Christ himself, and thenceforth that of all Catholic clergy. Pennington, *Pope and Bishops*, 39, finds in Innocent's *Register* that he identified himself with the kingly as well as the priestly role of Melchisedech, an association not made in the sermons.

94. *Provisio.* See Geoffrey Barraclough, *Papal Provisions* (Oxford: 1935; Westport, CT: Greenwood Press, 1971). Connie Mae Munk, 1:212, explains: "Papal provision of benefices refers to the right of the Pope to confer a benefice directly without the consent of and even in opposition to the ordinary electors, but in this sermon the provision concerns papal provision to a bishopric." Pennington, *Pope and Bishops*, 123, places Innocent within the developing theory and practice regarding papal provisions of episcopal benefices, i.e., appointing a bishop directly, without consent of or even in opposition to the electors.

95. *BL Add.: iusticie renitentibus iniuste.*

96. *BL Add.: tenentur.*

97. "Accepto" is the verbal consent given by a cardinal in acknowledging his election as Pope. Once this verbal assent is freely given the *electus* is the valid Pope. In the marriage metaphor as Innocent uses it, this acceptance is comparable to that given by bride and groom when they say "I will" in the marriage ceremony.

98. *BL Add.* Munk, 1:213, cites Innocent's distinction as "taken from canon law" and identifies the canons.

99. 2 Cor. 11:2.

100. 1 Tim. 2:8.

101. 1 Tim. 1:5. *BL Add.* quotes in full.

102. Mt. 25:1–13. The parable of the "Wise and Foolish Virgins," attendants at the wedding procession. Christ refers to himself as a bridegroom in Mt. 9:15, and to his second coming as a wedding feast in Mt. 22:1–14.

103. Lk. 12:37.

## Notes to Sermon Four

1. *Glossa* 4:18. An understanding of "salt" as it was known to medieval audiences may be gathered from Robert P. Multhauf, *Neptune's Gift: A History of Common Salt* (Baltimore: Johns Hopkins, 1978), 20–61 *et passim*, and from S. A. M. Adshead, *Salt and Civilization* (New York: St. Martin, 1992), 3–98. For discussions of the exegetical problems of the biblical parable, see James E. Latham, *The Religious Symbolism of Salt* (Paris: Beauchesne, 1982), 189–242.

2. Lev. 2:13; Num. 18:19.

3. Some sense of the medieval understanding of the geology and chemistry involved can be gleaned from the mid-thirteenth century Albertus Magnus, *Book of Minerals*, trans. Dorothy Wycoff (Oxford: Clarendon Press, 1967), 237–42.

4. D. 40 c. 6.

5. In Sermon Two Innocent himself substitutes "earth" for "it."

6. Mt. 5:13.

7. Innocent uses the term *argument* in its technical sense as the process of deducing a conclusion from valid propositions. The syllogistic sequence also provides the sermon's structure. Jean Chatillon, "La Bible dans les écoles du XIIe siècle," *Le Moyen Age et la Bible*, ed. Pierre Riché and Guy Lobrichon (Paris: Beauchesne, 1984), 186, points to the Paris masters' interest in the historical interpretation of scripture and to the dense texture of biblical verses, particularly syllogisms, which "are hidden in Scripture as fish in the depth of the waters," *Expositio in Psalmos Selectos*, PL 172: 279 ("latent in sacra Scriptura, ut piscis in profunda aqua," attributed to Honorius of Autun).

8. *Glossa* on Mt. 5:13, PL 114: 91B.

9. Wis. 6:7, 6.

10. Juvenal, *Satires* 8.140–41. Translation ours. Cf. Loeb edition, 168.

11. Innocent is referring here to the seven gifts of the Holy Spirit (Is. 11:2, LXX) which are linked to the seven principal virtues (four philosophical and three theological).

12. Mt. 5:19.

13. Acts 1:1.

14. 1 Pet. 2:21–22.

15. 1 Pet. 2:22.

16. Ex. 28:35.

17. Mt. 23:4.

18. Lk. 4:23.

19. Mt. 7:5.

20. Rom. 2:21–22.

21. Lk. 12:49.

22. Song 8:7.

23. Prov. 18:4.

24. *Glossa* on Mt. 5:13, PL 114: 91B.

25. *Glossa* on Lk. 14:35, PL 114: 310C.

26. Job 6:6.

27. Tob. 6:6.

28. Ps. 106:34.

29. Mt. 24:45. Pericope for Sermon Two.

30. Gal. 5:17.

31. Gen. 3:17–18.

32. 1 Cor. 1:24.

33. Col. 4:6.

34. 2 Kg. 2:19–21.

35. Rom. 7:12

36. 2 Cor. 3:6.

37. The synagogue symbolizes Judaism, which, according to Christian teaching, was fulfilled only by Christ: e.g. Mt. 5:17–18; Mk. 4:49; Lk. 22:37; Jn. 19:28; Acts 13:33.

38. Acts 9:15.

39. Mt. 9:17.

40. Mk. 9:49.

41. Jn. 6:64.

42. Jn. 2:1–10.

43. Ex. 34:34; 2 Cor 3:6; 2 Cor 3:12–18.

44. 1 Cor. 9:27.

45. Jn. 11:39, the body of the dead Lazarus, Sermon 10 *De sanctis*, 495D.

46. Ps. 118:120.

47. Gal. 5:24.

48. Sir.1:27.

49. Scriptural reference unknown.

50. Jg. 9:45.

51. Heb. 11:33.

52. Jer. 1:10.

53. Lev. 2:13.

54. *Vanitas*, literally "emptiness."

55. Rom. 8:20.

56. Eccles. 1:2.

57. Ps. 38:6.

58. Ps. 4:3.

59. Ps. 61:10.

60. Ps. 77:33.

61. Job 14:1–2.

62. Rom. 1:21.

63. Ps. 11:3.

64. Eccles.1:14. Jerome gives Solomon as the author, PL 113: 1115D.

65. Cf. Eccles. 1:15

66. *BL Add.: ad calorem, quidam solummodo.*

67. Dan. 13:8. In *De quad.*, PL 217: 957D, Innocent remarks that the three old judges broke the canons of "justness:" no integrity of mind (malice their object), no truth to facts (they lied), no observance of the law. In Sermon 11 *De tempore*, PL 217:

364A, these elders are called hypocrites, who "simulate sanctity without, but conserve iniquity within, not wishing to appear what they are, but wishing to appear who they are not" ("extra simulant sanctitatem, sed intus conservant iniquitatem: nolentes apparere quod sunt, sed volentes apparere qui non sunt").

68. Behemoth is described in Job 40:10–19, suggestively as a counter to the man with belted loins. His watery places were long associated with the dissolution of laziness and physical luxuriousness. Gregory, *Moralia*, PL 76: 678–79. Innocent, Sermon 15 *De tempore*, PL 217: 383A: "Watery places are luxurious hearts in which the (f)lux of concupiscence, abounds" ("Aquosa loca, sunt corda luxuriosa, in quibus concupiscentiae luxus exuberat").

69. Job 24:19. See also Sermon 15 *De tempore*, PL 217: 384D, for discussion of spiritual and carnal lusts.

70. Ps. 57:9. See Sermon 16 *De tempore*, PL 217: 386C.

71. Gen. 49:4. Reuben's incest with his father's concubine (Gen. 35:22) denied him the pre-eminence as firstborn in Jacob's blessing: a double portion of the inheritance, power over his brothers, and priesthood. That Innocent's categories are not rigid is apparent in that Reuben's lust can be taken also as a spiritual envy of his father's place with the concubine.

72. Lev. 4:3.

73. Rom. 14:4.

74. D. 21 c. 7 (Friedberg, 1:71) which this and the previous two sentences together paraphrase. Reportedly, Pope Marcellinus (296–304) had apostatized during the savage persecution under Diocletian, and the bishops who were called upon to try him would not. They cautioned that the case rested in the pontiff's own heart. Repenting his lapse, Marcellinus died a martyr. The account of the alleged incident is one of the Symmachian falsifications which seek to demonstrate the adage, "the first chair is judged by no one"; see *Synodi Sinuessanae de Marcellino papa*, PL 6: 11–20 and the *Encyclopedia of the Early Church*, s.v. "Marcellinus" and "Symmachus." Nevertheless, it exemplifies the principle of papal immunity from oversight also illustrated in D. 17 ante c. 7; D. 21 cc. 4, 7; C. 9 q. 3 cc.10–18; C. 17 q. 4 c. 30; see Brian Tierney, *Foundations of Conciliar Theory: The Contribution of the Medieval Canonists from Gratian to the Great Schism* (Cambridge: Cambridge University Press, 1955), 57. Cf. n. 80.

75. Cf. D. 40 c. 6, which contains the phrase, "he is to be judged by none, unless he has deviated from faith." The literature is large: Tierney, *Foundations*, 57–67, is basic; James M. Moynihan, *Papal Immunity and Liability in the Writings of the Medieval Canonists* (Rome: Gregorian University Press, 1961), 1–110, systematically goes through decretist doctrines on papal immunity, 1140–1220; Alfons M. Stickler, "Papal Infallibility—a Thirteenth Century Invention? Reflections on a Recent Book," *The Catholic Historical Review* 70 (1974): 431, points out the canonist tradition that the Pope cannot be judged except in questions of faith, noting that the Pope may personally become a heretic, "but as such he would place himself outside the church and would cease to be Pope." Kenneth Pennington, *Pope and Bishops*, 13–42, is particularly clear and indicates further readings.

76. Jn. 3:18.

77. Ezek. 18:21–28.

78. Lk. 15:3–7.

79. Lk. 15:8–10.

80. Cf. Lk. 15:10.

81. 2 Sam. 11–12.

82. *Principatum*, the foremost authority held by the Roman Pontiff; in Roman law a secular office, later the office of Pope; see Berger, s.v. *princeps, principatum*. Also, *major domo*, the service performed by the Pope overseeing the household of Christ; see Niermeyer, s.v., and cf. Sermon Two.

83. Lk. 22:32.

84. Gal. 5:6.

## Notes to Sermon Six

1. A description (c. 1180) of the church's *sancta* can be found in *Descriptio Lateranensis ecclesiae*, ed. Roberto Valentini and Guiseppe Zucchetti, *Codice Topografico della Città di Roma*, vol. 3 (Rome, 1946), 326–73.

2. Kuttner and Garcia, 130.

3. *Register* 16 no. 30, PL 216: 823–27.

4. John W. Baldwin, *Masters, Princes, and Merchants* 1: 373.

5. Lk. 22:16.

6. There is no way to know whether at the time of the council Innocent had a presentiment of his death. His health had always been poor, and at one point early in his pontificate he was so ill that reports of his death had circulated. As it happened, it was only a matter of months after the council that he did die on July 16, 1216, of the tertian fever which had plagued him for years.

7. *Glossa*, PL 114: 337. Linkage of the Israelite Passover with the Last Supper of Christ and with the apocalyptic Supper of the Lamb is noted in a marginal gloss to Lk. 22:16. The interlinear gloss provides a clear association of the paschal lamb with Christ, the Lamb of God, the title given him by John the Baptist in Jn. 1:29.

8. The eighteen-year record for which is to be found in Innocent's copious correspondence.

9. This investigative process was drawn from Roman and medieval civil law, and takes its name "inquisition" from the search for evidence in legal cases.

10. See Tanner 1:237–38, Constitutions 7 and 8.

11. As historians now know, "inquisitions" took place, but there was never "the" inquisition. See Edward Peters, *Inquisition* (New York: The Free Press, 1988), 12 and passim, and his account of the differences between such steps as Lateran IV took and the institutionalizing of inquisition by later authorities.

12. Wilhelm Imkamp, "Sermo Ultimus," 161, has noted this three-level gradient by which human souls, individually and collectively, can progress from the realm of their natural earthly condition, through the realm of grace received from God, and thence to the glory of seeing God face-to-face. This model informed much of Innocent's

world view, and occurs in a number of his sermons: 2 and 23 *De tempore*; 3, 4, 10, 20 *De sanctis*; and it is strongly implied in our Sermon Seven.

13. Innocent adds his own (non-Scriptural) ending to the pericope, Lk. 22:16.

14. Phil.1:21 and Mt. 26:42, a reference to Christ's agony in the garden of Gethsemane.

15. Lk. 22: 42.
16. Ps. 118:20.
17. Song 2:3.
18. 1 Pet. 2:11.
19. Sir. 23:5.
20. Lk. 22:1.
21. Lev. 23:5.
22. Lk. 22:7.
23. Jn. 18:28.
24. Jn. 13:1.
25. 1 Cor. 5:7.
26. Lk. 24:26.
27. Rom. 8:18.
28. Ex. 12:11.

29. 2 Kings 23:3; 2 Chr. 35:1. *Paralipomenon*, Greek meaning "things left out," is the Vulgate name for the two Hebrew books called Chronicles, which are supplements to the books of Kings. A full account of Josiah's reform of Israel is found in 2 Chr. 34.

30. Innocent here employs the magisterial plural "our" for the only time in these sermons *De diversis*. The effect is to announce the official opening of Lateran Council IV.

31. Mt. 18:20.

32. *status*, "condition." The term "status of the Church" *(status Ecclesiae)* embraced "not only the faith and welfare of the members of the church, but also the rule of church law, the ecclesiastical *ordo* that was necessary for governing the Church and . . . maintaining the *status Ecclesiae*"; see Gaines Post, "Copyists' Errors and the Problem of Papal Dispensations 'Contra Statutum Generale Ecclesiae' or 'Contra Statum Generalem Ecclesiae' According to the Decretists and Decretalists ca. 1150–1234," *Studia Gratiana* 9 (1966): 364. Yves M.-J. Congar, "Status Ecclesiae," *Studia Gratiana* 15 (1972): 3–31, has traced the history of the term *status Ecclesiae*, including the relationship between the Pope's responsibility of caring for the good order of church and society *(sollicitudo)* and his use of power *(plenitudo potestatis)* to foster that aim. In the context of Lateran IV the phrase sets up the Pope's effort at reform, i.e. bringing the actual state of the church into conformity with its ideal state: health, stability, peace, common utility, good of the whole.

33. Jerusalem as grieving mother was an age-old Judeo-Christian image. Innocent composes her *planctus*, plaint, so as to quote and otherwise echo the meanings of *transitus* and *pasch* found in the Holy Week liturgy: Ps. 21:1–9 and 18b–19, part of the Tract for Palm Sunday, and passages from the opening of Lamentations found in Matins

for Holy Thursday and Good Friday, with his own phrases modeled on the Reproaches, or *Improperia*.

34. Agar (Hagar), Abraham's concubine and the handmaid (slave) of Sara, Abraham's wife. Abraham's and Agar's son, Ismael, was understood to be the father of the Arabs, thus "Agarenes."

35. Mattathias, of the priestly line of Yehoyarib, rebelled against the Seleucid Antiochus IV, who in 167 B.C.E. set up the "abomination of desolation" in the temple and forced Jews to violate Torah. Mattathias and his sons after him fought to free and cleanse the temple, and finally free Jerusalem itself. See Jonathan A. Goldstein, *I Maccabees: A New Translation with Introduction and Commentary*, Anchor Bible (Garden City, N.Y.: Doubleday, 1976), 161–74 *et passim*.

36. Ezek. 9:3–4. As the last letter of the Hebrew alphabet *Tau* was thought by some exegetes to represent the fulfillment of the Law; others thought that *Tau*, as the first letter of Torah, represented the totality of the Law; see Origen, *Selecta in Ezechielem*, PG 13: 801. In Jewish exegesis *Tau* was used as a mark of separation or protection, as in Ex. 12:23. Because it resembled the shape of a cross, early Christians saw it as a sign of Christ's cross, e.g., Jerome, *Commentarium in Ezechielem*, PL 25: 88. Innocent had previously mentioned it as marking the foreheads of Crusaders; *Register* 5 no. 46, PL 214: 1012. *De Mysteriis*, PL 217: 840, notes that it stands in the words *Te igitur* at the beginning of the Canon of the Mass, the most sacred part of the ritual. In 1212 the *Tau* had been adopted as an emblem by the boy Nicholas, leader of the tragic Children's Crusade; Dana C. Munro, "The Children's Crusade," *American Historical Review* 19 (1914): 516–24. Later St. Francis of Assisi took the *Tau* as his personal signature, perhaps as a pledge of his commitment to the reforms of Lateran IV; Damien Vorreux, *Un Symbole Franciscain: Le Tau* (Paris: Editions Franciscaines, 1977), 13–20.

37. Ezek. 9:4,5.

38. Job 1:1.

39. Eccles. 9:8.

40. In linen making flax stalks are softened in water (macerated) then pounded so as to leave only true flax, which is then combed, and the fibers are spun into yarn. The highest grade of linen is that which is soaked in the purest water and carefully macerated; see Patricia Baines, *Linen: Hand Spinning and Weaving* (B.T. Batsford: London, 1989) and *Anchor Bible Dictionary*, vol. 2, s.v. "Flora," "Textiles." Similarly, *contrition* shares with *threshing* a common root *\*tere*, culling husks from grain; see *The American Heritage Dictionary of Indo-European Roots*, rev. and ed. Calvert Watkins (Boston: Houghton Mifflin, 1985), s.v.

41. Ps. 44:2, the phenomenon of inspiration of the human author by the Holy Spirit. Innocent explains: "For just as ink from a writing horn marks parchment by means of a pen, thus the Holy Spirit, through the tongue of the Prophet, filled the human heart with the knowledge of the truth concerning the secret of the Divinity." See Munk's translation, *De quad.* 2:76.

42. Ex. 12:11. Girding, in context a figure of self-discipline, also evokes the figure of "passover": Israelites girded their loins in preparation to flee Egypt. This reference links the Ezekiel passage to the Passover theme of this sermon.

43. Ps. 25:2. *De mysteriis*, PL 217: 783, identifies this act of girding or girdling the loins as signifying chastity, the restraint of concupiscence.

44. Lk. 4:23.

45. Rom. 2:21–22.

46. Lk. 12:35.

47. Mk. 15:26; Lk. 23:38; Jn. 19:19–22.

48. Ex. 12: 21–24.

49. Gal. 5:24.

50. Gal. 6:14.

51. 2 Cor. 11:29. Innocent, *In septem psalmos*, PL 217: 1045B: "[the good man] is saddened and sorrows when he sees the unjust sinning, according to what the Apostle says . . . for the sins of neighbors are the frying pans of the just" (Ps. 101:4); the Latin reads, "plus tristatur et condolet, cum turbari cernit injustum, secundum quod dicit Apostolus: Quis infirmatur, et ego non infirmor? quis scandalizatur, et ego non uror? Nam peccata proximorum frixorium sunt justorum." The same work, PL 217: 1082D–1085, also has an intense and moving *divisio* on *et ossa mea sicut in frixorio confrixa sunt*, "And my bones have been fried in the frying pan" (Ps. 101:4). Cf. *Glossa*, PL 114: 567–68, and Peter Lombard, *Commentarium in Psalmos*, PL 191: 907.

52. *speculator*. This examiner is the bishop, *episcopus*, the one who oversees or superintends the welfare of his diocese. In *De mysteriis*, PL 217: 777–78, Innocent supports this identification by citing Ezekiel 3:17, in which God appoints the prophet as a watchman or sentinel who warns the city of approaching danger, i.e., divine judgment. For other Biblical references see Is. 52:8; 56:10; Jer. 6:17; Hos. 9:8.

53. Ps 2:6 and Mt. 5:14.

54. The documents of Lateran IV describe the cautions and safeguards surrounding such investigations and the charity which should precede any corrections of moral faults; see Tanner 1:237–39.

55. Is. 5:20. This admonition is part of the consecration ceremony for bishops.

56. Ezek. 13:19.

57. Ezek. 8:8–16.

58. These symbolic of numbers and of the six ages of the world, both well known to medieval writers, owe much to Augustine, who drew upon an inherited symbolism based on the six days of creation; see Gerhart B. Ladner, *The Idea of Reform: Its Impact on Christian Thought and Action in the Age of the Fathers* (Cambridge, MA: Harvard University Press, 1959), 222–38. Augustine configured the six ages as "from Adam to Noah, from Noah to Abraham, from Abraham to David, from David to the Babylonian Captivity, from the Captivity to Christ, from Christ to the world's end." See Ladner, 225. Cf. also J. A. Burrows, *The Ages of Man: A Study in Medieval Writing and Thought* (Oxford: Clarendon Press, 1988), 79–92, 199–200.

59. "Pontifical" here refers primarily to the power of bishops, whom Innocent is addressing. It also would include the Pope, the Supreme Pontiff.

60. Ps. 100:8.

61. Ps. 7:13–14.

62. Rev. 3:7 transposes the description of Eliakim, a prophetic figure pictured in Is. 22:22 as majordomo of the palace, with the robes and key of the House of David, into the figure of Christ. Innocent thus evokes his own position as "servant constituted over the household," and Christ's "serving" at the banquet of the eternal passover. The "keys" inevitably indicate Peter in his historical role of Christ's Vicar and High Priest and also the commission to bind and to loosen (Mt. 16:19). This verse, chanted in the "O Antiphons" before Christmas, annually announces the teaching and judicial authority of Christ and his vicars.

63. Rev. 7:3.

64. Ezek. 9:5.

65. *personarum acceptio*, meaning "partiality" or "favoritism" in Jas. 2:1, 1 Pet. 1:17; cf. Jas. 2:9, Acts 10:34.

66. Ex. 32:26–28.

67. Deut. 32:39.

68. Ezek. 9:6.

69. 1 Pet. 4:17.

70. Lev. 4:3.

71. Jn. 5:19.

72. Mt. 10:25.

73. Hos. 4:9.

74. Is. 23:4. Peter of Blois, PL 207: 734C, glossing "Blush with shame": "Let priests blush when lay people, who are immersed in the sea of this world, are found more holy than they themselves" ("Erubescant sacerdotes, si sacratioris vitae inveniuntur laici, qui hujus mundi fluctibus sunt immersi").

75. Lk. 12:37.

76. Ps. 65:12.

77. Mt. 14:16.

78. Acts 10:13.

79. Ps. 105:28.

80. Deut. 32:42.

81. Jn. 4:32.

82. Ps. 101:10, the ashes of mourning and repentance. See Es. 4:1 and 3, Job 42:6, Is. 58:5, Dan. 9:3, Mt.11:21, Lk. 10:13.

83. Jn. 6:58.

84. Lk. 14:15.

## Notes to Sermon Seven

1. Mitchell Dahood, *Psalms II: 51–100*, The Anchor Bible (Garden City, N.Y.: Doubleday, 1968), 133.

2. Augustine, for instance, turned an expert grammatical eye to this text and had difficulty telling whether to parse the sentence with what precedes it or with what follows; he gives several readings, never arriving at a determination for the verse; yet he

comes to an overall view of it as christological; see *Exposition on the Book of Psalms*, in A Select Library of the Nicene and Post-Nicene Fathers of the Christian Church (Grand Rapids, Michigan: Eerdmans, 1974 [reprint of 1888]), 290–92.

3. Dt. 10:8, 21:15: Num. 1:53,18:6.

4. Jos. 18:7; 13:14, 33; 1 Chr. 6:64–65.

5. Dt. 32:8–9.

6. Ps. 16.

7. The Biblical resonances of this concept are extensive and enriching to Innocent's point here. In addition to the above direct application to the Levites, the notion of "lots" extends to the casting of lots as a means of discerning God's will. The *Urim* and *Thummim* of the High Priest's vestments were of this sort. The Hebraic division of property was arrived at by casting lots, the assigned property then becoming an inheritance. It was also a means of selecting men for special office (1 Chr. 24:4–5, 31). After Judas's suicide, the apostles themselves cast lots to select a replacement for his share in the ministry of Christ (Acts 1:26). Indeed, the money Judas had received for his betrayal of Christ, thus forfeiting his share in the ministry, was spent to buy a (p)lot of land, another inheritance (Mt. 27: 6–10; Acts 1:18–19). Supporting the conceptual associations, etymologically *merit* and *clergy*, although different lexemes, share meanings of "being set aside in some fashion." *Merit* descends from Indo-European *\*(s)mer-*, to obtain a share of something. *Clergy* descends from Greek *kleros*, meaning "lot" or "allotment," from Indo-European *\*kel-*, "that which is cut off." See *The American Heritage Dictionary of Indo-European Roots*, s.v.

8. *The American Heritage Dictionary of Indo-European Roots*, s.v. *\*pet-*.

9. Where we use "pinions," the Latin text of Ps. 67:14 has *posteriora ejus*, "her back" or "her back feathers."

10. Acts 1:1 and 1 Pet. 2:21–22, quoting Is. 53:9.

11. Ex. 28:34–35.

12. *operatio*, which Innocent associates with perseverance; ideally it accompanies good judgment, *intellectum*; see *In septem psalmos*, PL 217: 1022A–C.

13. Ex. 28:35.

14. *pietas*.

15. Ps. 83:12.

16. The "sleep" of spiritual death is *culpa*, transgressions committed by individuals; the "sleep" of physical death, however, is *poena*, the universal condition of original sin.

17. Jn. 11:11.

18. 1 Thess. 4:12.

19. Ps. 40:9.

20. Eph. 5:14.

21. Ps. 12:4.

22. Prov. 6:9–11.

23. Ps. 75:6.

24. Mt. 26:45.

25. Song 5:2.

26. *perfectio*, completing or finishing, i.e., fulfilling potential; the opposite is *corruptio*, extinction or annihilation.

27. Ps. 36:27.

28. By reading PL's *intentione* as "intensione" (they sound alike), Innocent's sentence is a direct quote from William of Conches: "Est enim somnus quies virtutum animalium cum intensione naturalium." See *Glossae super platonem*, ed. Edouard Jeanneau (Paris: Vrin, 1965), 241.

29. The "divine precepts," i.e., the "Law," include the Ten Commandments and other rules as particularly found in Torah. "The administration of the sacraments of the church" is a phrase describing the duties of priesthood in Leviticus; see *Glossa*, PL 113: 295B.

30. Ps. 94:11.

31. Ps. 81:5.

32. Hos. 4:6

33. Is. 5:13.

34. Ps. 35:4–5.

35. 1 Cor. 2:8.

36. Mt. 13:11–13.

37. Job 1:13. *Glossa*, PL 113: 745B, quoting Gregory, *Moralia*, PL 75: 578D and 589A on the special obligation of the clergy (oxen) to acquire and exemplify learning and charity to the people. "Oxen plowing" was also a figure of the process of writing with stylus upon wax and parchment, thus of learning and scholarship; see Ernst R. Curtius, *European Literature and the Latin Middle Ages*, trans. Willard R. Trask (Princeton, NJ: Princeton University Press, 1967), 313.

38. Ps. 118:16. The clergy's singing is the chanting of the Divine Office.

39. Mt. 5:14.

40. Mt. 6:22.

41. Mt. 5:13, pericope for Sermon Four.

42. Rom. 12:1.

43. 1 Pet. 3:15.

44. Ex. 28:30. *Manifestatio et veritas* is one of the Latin translations of the Septuagint Greek terms which translate the ancient Hebrew terms *Urim* and *Thummim;* Vulgate has *doctrina et veritas*. Gratian, e.g., uses *manifestatio*, D. 36 c. 2 (Friedberg 1:134).

45. Mal. 2:7.

46. Mt. 15:14.

47. Ps. 120:4.

48. Is. 29:13.

49. Ps. 61:5.

50. Mt. 6:6.

51. Eccles.10:1, a much used explication of distractions in prayer; see *In septem psalmos*, PL 217: 1038C.

52. Mt. 6:7.

53. 1 Tim. 1:5.

54. Moses in Ex. 8:12, 15:25, 17:4, and Num. 12:13; Susanna in Dan. 13:42. Innocent

commends Susanna's "clamor," arising from a believing heart; see *In septem psalmos*, PL 217: 1081D.

55. Ps. 36:4. This passage from "Some pray so negligently" through "the requests of your heart" is found with minor variations in Sermon 11 *De tempore*, PL 217: 364C–365D. This passage in slightly longer form reappears in an Ottobeuron MS of 1246, which Richard Trexler assigns to Peter the Chanter. Since Ottobeuron is unique in quoting this passage, and since Innocent wrote after Peter the Chanter, it is not clear whether Innocent quotes Peter, or whether Innocent's passage has been inserted into this one copy of *De oratione et speciebus illius*, lines 1150–86. See *The Christian at Prayer*, 200–202, and statement, p. 18, "I will argue that Peter the Chanter did write the *De penitentia* [which includes this prayer manual], but that it can be dangerous to assign particular statements to him."

56. Eph. 5:19.

57. Ps. 7:10.

58. 1 Sam.1:13. Anna, being barren, vowed that if God gave her a son she would dedicate him to the Lord; the son she bore, Samuel, became a prophet.

59. Ps. 4:5.

60. Ps. 50:19, reminiscent of Sermon One, and the sacrifice required for the sins of priests.

61. Ps. 65:17.

62. Jer. 48:10.

63. Ps. 2:11.

64. Lk. 22:19.

65. 1 Cor. 11:26.

66. 1 Cor. 11:29.

67. Is. 56:10.

68. Ezek. 13:18.

69. Ezek. 13:10.

70. Lam. 2:14.

71. Is. 58:1.

72. Acts 20:26–27.

73. Is. 6:5.

74. Mt. 14:1–12.

75. Eph. 4:26; Ps. 4:5.

76. Ps. 68:10; Jn. 2:17.

77. Num. 25.

78. Lk. 10:30–36.

79. Num. 17:16–26; Ex. 16:32–34.

80. Sir. 10:9–10.

81. Jesus Ben Sirach, now called Ben Sira or Siracides, author of the Book of Sirach, formerly called the Book of Ecclesiasticus, the "Preacher"; see Patrick W. Skeehand and Alexander A. Di Lella, *The Wisdom of Ben Sira*, The Anchor Bible (New York: Doubleday, 1987), 3–20.

82. 1 Tim. 6:9–10.

83. Eph. 5:5.

84. Mic. 3:11.

85. Prov. 27:20.

86. Prov. 30:15. *Glossa*, PL 113: 1113B, identifies the leech's "daughters" as avarice and luxury.

87. Juvenal, *Satires* 14.139. Translation ours. Cf. Loeb edition, 274.

88. 1 Jn. 2:17.

89. Ps. 48:17–18.

90. Ps. 61:11.

91. Deut. 23:25.

92. Sir. 19:2.

93. Prov. 7:27.

94. Prov. 5:3–4.

95. Job 40:11.

96. Cf. Horace, *Odes* 1.19.11 and 2.13.17, describing the Parthian victory gained by strategic retreat, an example cited by Alan of Lille, *Summa*, PL 210: 122. Innocent also quotes this in *De miseriis*, PL 217: 725C.

97. 1 Sam. 21:4.

98. This is a listing, in order, of the three theological virtues, the four cardinal virtues, and the seven gifts of the Holy Spirit.

99. Ps. 118:20.

100. Mt. 5:16.

101. Rev. 22: 17.

102. Ps. 15:5.

103. Ps. 135:21–22.

104. Ps. 118:111.

105. Ps. 15:6.

106. 1 Jn. 2:15.

107. 2 Cor. 3:6.

108. Mt. 5:12.

109. Song 6:8. The dove of the Song is identified in the marginal glosses as a figure of the church, taken from Augustine. Innocent's exegesis in this passage closely parallels the *Glossa*.

110. Is. 60:8.

111. Ps. 11:7.

112. Song 5:12.

113. Ps. 17:11.

114. Ps. 54:7.

115. Ezek. 1:9. The four winged figures in Ezekiel's dreams have wings that touch each other and have long been taken as figures of the four evangelists, each with its own distinct character (lion, ox, man, eagle), but joined in overarching meaning; see, e.g., Gregory, *Moralia* 29.31.7.

116. Cf. Job 39:13.

117. Ps. 128:3.

118. Rev. 21:4.

119. The phrase "rest after labor" echoes the passover metaphor of the ending of Sermon Six, "that we may passover from labor to rest."

120. Mt. 13:43.

## Notes to Epilogue

1. Dante, *Divine Comedy*, "Paradiso," Canto 11, 92f.

2. It was in a war between Perugia and Assisi that Francis had been taken captive and imprisoned. While being held prisoner he contracted the illness that seems to have triggered his "conversion" to sanctity.

3. James of Vitry, letter to Bohmer Analekten, 65f. Cited by Tillmann, 315 n. 125.

4. V. Cramer, *Die Kreuzzugspredigt zur Befreiung des Hl. Landes 1095–1270*, Studien zur Geschichte und Charakteristik der Kreuzzugspropaganda (1939), 191 n. 2.

5. See the peroration of Sermon Two and the summoning of the General Council [Lateran Four] in *Register* 16, no. 30, PL 216: 824A ("reformatio universalis Ecclesiae").

6. *The Life of St. Francis (Legenda Maior)*, trans. Ewert Cousins (New York: Paulist Press, 1978), 246.

7. Ibid. 214. Today's pilgrims to Francis's hermitage still wear the wooden *Tau* as evidence and symbol of their trek.

8. Dante, *Divine Comedy*, Canto 11, 110.

# BIBLIOGRAPHY

Abraham ibn Ezra. *The Commentary of Abraham ibn Ezra on the Pentateuch. Volume 3: Leviticus.* Trans. Jay F. Schachter. Hoboken, NJ: Ktav Publishing House, 1986.

Adshead, S. A. M. *Salt and Civilization.* New York: St. Martin, 1992.

Alan of Lille. *In distinctionibus dictionum theologicalium.* PL 210.

Alan of Lille. *Summa de arte praedicatoria.* PL 210. *The Art of Preaching.* Trans. Gillian R. Evans. Kalamazoo: Cistercian Publications, 1991.

Albertus Magnus. *Book of Minerals.* Trans. Dorothy Wycoff. Oxford: Clarendon Press, 1967.

Alighieri, Dante. *The Divine Comedy.* Trans. and comment. John D. Sinclair. New York: Oxford University Press, 1992.

*The American Heritage Dictionary of Indo-European Roots.* Rev. and ed. Calvert Watkins. Boston: Houghton Mifflin, 1985.

*Anchor Bible Dictionary.* Garden City, N.Y.: Doubleday, 1992.

*The Anchor Bible with Introductions, Translations, and Notes.* Garden City, NY: Doubleday, 1964–.

Augustine. *De civitate Dei.* PL 41. *The City of God.* Trans. Marcus Dods. New York: Modern Library, 1950.

———. *De doctrina Christiana.* Trans. D. W. Robertson, Jr. Indianapolis: Bobbs Merrill, 1978.

———. *Exposition on the Book of Psalms.* Trans. A. Cleveland Cox. A Select Library of the Nicene and Post-Nicene Fathers of the Christian Church. Ed. Philip Schaff. Grand Rapids, Michigan: Eerdmans, 1974 [reprint of 1888].

Baines, Patricia. *Linen: Hand Spinning and Weaving.* B. T. Batsford: London, 1989.

Baldwin, John W. *Masters, Princes, and Merchants: the Social Views of Peter the Chanter and his Circle.* 2 vols. Princeton: Princeton University Press, 1970.

Barraclough, Geoffrey. *Papal Provisions.* Oxford: 1935; Westport, CT: Greenwood Press, 1971.

Bede. "Life of St. Cuthbert." *The Age of Bede.* Trans. J. F.Webb. Ed. D. H. Farmer. Harmondsworth and New York: Penguin Books, 1965; repr. ed. 1983.

Benson, Robert I.. *The Bishop-Elect: A Study in Medieval Ecclesiastical Office.* Princeton, NJ: Princeton University Press, 1968.

———. "Plenitudo Potestatis: Evolution of a Formula from Gregory IV to Gratian." *Studia Gratiana* 11 (1967): 104–217.

Berger, Adolf. *Encyclopedic Dictionary of Roman Law.* Transactions of the American Philosophical Society, n.s., 43 pt. 2. Philadelphia, 1953.

Bernard of Clairvaux. *De consideratione.* In *Sancti Bernardi Opera,* vol. 3. Ed. Jean Leclercq and Henri Rochais. Rome: Editiones Cistercienses, 1963. *Five Books on Consideration: Advice to a Pope.* Trans. John D. Anderson and Elizabeth T. Kennan. Kalamazoo: Cistercian Publications, 1976.

*Biblia Latina cum glossa ordinaria: Facsimile reprint of the editio princeps of Adolph Busch of Strassburg 1480/81.* Intro. Karlfried Froehlich and Margaret T. Gibson. 4 vols. Turnhout: Brepols, 1992.

Blaise, Albert. *Le vocabulaire latin des principaux thèmes liturgiques.* Turnhout: Brepols, 1966.

Bonaventure. *The Soul's Journey into God, The Tree of Life, The Life of St. Francis.* Trans. with intro. by Ewert Cousins. New York: Paulist Press, 1978.

Burrows, J. A. *The Ages of Man: A Study in Medieval Writing and Thought.* Oxford: Clarendon Press, 1988.

Chatillon, Jean. "La Bible dans les écoles du XIIe siècle." In *Le Moyen Age et la Bible.* Ed. Pierre Riche and Guy Lobrichon, 163–97. Paris: Beauchesne, 1984.

*Codice Baberini Latino 2733.* Ed. Reto Niggl. Rome: Biblioteca Apostolica Vaticana, 1972.

Colish, Marcia L. *The Mirror of Language: A Study in the Medieval Theory of Knowledge.* Lincoln: University of Nebraska Press, 1968.

———. *Peter Lombard.* 2 vols. Leiden: E. J. Brill, 1994.

Congar, Yves M.-J. "Cephas-Céphalè-Caput." *Revue du moyen âge Latin* 8 (1952): 5–42.

———. "Ecce constitui te super gentes et regna (Jer. 1:10) 'In Geschichte und Gegenwart.'" In *Theologie in Geschichte und Gegenwart: Michael Schmaus zum sechzigten Geburtstag dargebracht von sein Freunden and Schülern,* ed. Johann Auer and Herman Volk, Munich: Karl Zink Verlag, 1957: 671–95.

———. "Homo spiritualis: Usage juridique et politique d'un terme d'anthropologie chrétienne." In *Aus Kirche und Reich: Studien zu Theologie, Politique und Recht im Mittelalter,* 1–10. Ed. Hubert Mordek. Sigmaringen: Jan Thorbecke Verlag, 1983.

———. "Status Ecclesiae." *Studia Gratiana* 15 (1972): 3–31.

Cramer, V. *Die Kreuzzugspredigt zur Befreiung des Hl. Landes 1095–1270.* Studien zur Geschichte und Charakteristik der Kreuzzugspropaganda, 1939.

Curtius, Ernst R. *European Literature and the Latin Middle Ages.* Trans. Willard R. Trask. Princeton, NJ: Princeton University Press, 1967.

Dahood, Mitchell. *Psalms II: 51–100.* The Anchor Bible. Garden City, NY: Doubleday, 1968.

Deferrari, Roy J. *A Latin-English Dictionary of St. Thomas Aquinas.* Boston: St. Paul Editions, 1960.

Denzinger, H. *The Sources of Catholic Dogma.* Trans. Roy J. Deferrari from the Thirtieth Edition of Henry Denzinger's *Enchiridion Symbolorum.* St. Louis: Herder, 1957.

*Descriptio Lateranensis ecclesiae.* Ed. Roberto Valentini and Giuseppe Zucchetti. In *Codice Topografico della Città di Roma,* 326–73.

*Encyclopedia of the Early Church.* Ed. Angelo Di Berardino. Trans. Adrian Walford. With foreword and notes by W. H. C. Frend. Institutum Augustinianum. NY: Oxford University Press, 1992. S.v. "Synodi Sinuessanae de Marcellino papa."

Foreville, Raymonde. *Le Pape Innocent III et la France*. Päpste und Papsttum 26. Stuttgart: Hiersemann, 1992.

Friedberg, Emil, ed. *Corpus iuris canonici*. 2 vols. Leipzig: Tauchnitz, 1879; repr. ed., Graz: Akademische Druck u. Verlagsanstalt, 1959.

Froehlich, Karlfried. "Saint Peter, Papal Primacy, and the Exegetical Tradition, 1150–1300." In *Religious Roles of the Papacy: Ideals and Realities*, 4–44. Ed. Christopher Ryan. Toronto: Pontifical Institute of Mediaeval Studies, 1989.

Gaudemet, Jean. "Le symbolisme du mariage entre l'évêque et son église et ses consequences juridiques." In *Droit de l'église et vie sociale au moyen age*, 110–23. Northampton, Vermont: Variorum Reprints, 1985; repr. ed., 1989.

*Gesta Innocentii PP. III*. PL 214, xvi–ccxxviii.

*Glossa Ordinaria*. PL 113, 114.

Goldstein, Jonathan A. *1 Maccabees: A New Translation with Introduction and Commentary*. The Anchor Bible. Garden City, NY: Doubleday, 1976.

*Gratian: The Treatise on Laws (Decretum DD. 1–20)*. Trans. Augustine Thompson. *With the Ordinary Gloss*. Trans. James Gordley. Intro. Katherine Christensen. Washington, D.C.: The Catholic University of America Press, 1993.

*Gregory of Tours: the History of the Franks*. Trans. Lewis Thorpe. Harmondsworth and Baltimore: Penguin Books, 1974.

Gregory I. *Moralia*. PL 76–79.

Gregory I. *Liber Regulae Pastoralis*. Gregory the Great. *Pastoral Care*. Trans. and annotated Henry Davis. Westminster, MD: Newman Press, 1950.

Guibert of Nogent. *Liber quo ordine sermo fieri debeat*. PL 156. Miller, Joseph M. "Guibert DeNogent's 'Liber Quo Ordone Sermo Fieri Debeat:' a Translation of the Earliest Modern Speech Textbook. *Today's Speech* 17 (1969): 45–56.

Hamilton, Bernard. "The Albigensian Crusade." In *Monastic Reform, Catharism and the Crusades 900–1300*, VIII. London: Variorum Reprints, 1974; repr. ed., 1979.

Heaney, Seamus. *The Development of the Sacramentality of Marriage from Anselm of Laon to Thomas Aquinas*. Washington, D.C.: The Catholic University of America Press, 1963.

Horace. *De arte poetica*. Loeb Classical Library. Cambridge, MA: Harvard University Press, 1926.

———. *Odes* 1.19.11 and 2.13.17. Loeb Classical Library. Cambridge, MA: Harvard University Press, 1927.

Imkamp, Wilhelm. *Das Kirchenbild Innocenz' III (1198–1216)*. Päpste und Papsttum 22. Stuttgart: Hiersemann, 1983.

———. "'Pastor et sponsus:' Elemente einer Theologie des bischöflichen Amtes bei Innocenz III." In *Aus Kirche und Reich: Studien zu Theologie, Politik und Recht im Mittelalter*, 285–94. Festschrift für Friedrich Kempf. Ed. Hubert Mordek. Sigmaringen: Jan Thorbecke Verlag, 1983.

———. "Sermo Ultimus, quem facit Dominus Innocentius papa tercius in Lateranensi concilio generali." *Römische Quartalsschrift* 70 (1975): 149–78.

Innocent III. *Commentarium in septem psalmos penitentiales*. PL 217.

———. *De miseria condicionis humane*. PL 217.

———. *De missarum mysteriis*. PL 217.

———. *De quadripartita specie nuptiarum.* PL 217.

———. *Die Register Innocenz' III. Pontifikatsjahr, 1198/99.* Ed. Othmar Hageneder and Anton Haidacher. Graz-Köln: Verlag Hermann Böhlaus, 1964.

———. *Regestum Innocentii III papae super negotio Romani imperii.* Ed. Friedrich Kempf. Miscellanea Historiae Pontificiae 12. Rome: Pontificia Universite Gregoriana, 1947.

Jacqueline, Bernard. *Episcopat et papauté chez saint Bernard de Clairvaux.* Saint-Lo: Editions Henri Jacqueline, 1975.

Jasper, Detlev. *Das Papstwahldekret von 1059: Überlieferung und Textgestalt.* Sigmaringen: J. Thorbecke, 1986.

Jerome. *Commentarium in Ezechielem.* PL 25.

John Chrysostom. *In Isaiam.* PG 56.

John of Paris. *On Royal and Papal Power.* Trans. James A. Watt. Toronto: Pontifical Institute of Mediaeval Studies, 1971.

Juvenal. *Satires.* In *Juvenal and Persius.* Loeb Classical Library. Cambridge, MA: Harvard University Press, 1940.

Kempf, Friedrich. "Innocent III." In *Das Papsttum I: Von den Anfängen bis zu den Päpsten in Avignon.* Ed. Martin Greschat. Stuttgart: Verlag W. Kohlhammer, 1985: 196–207.

Kempf, Friedrich. *Papsttum und Kaisertum bei Innocenz III.* Rome: Pontificia Universitas Gregoriana, 1954.

Kennedy, Gerald Thomas. *St. Paul's Conception of the Priesthood of Melchisedech: An Historico-Exegetical Investigation.* Washington, D.C.: The Catholic University of America Press, 1951.

Krautheimer, Richard. *Rome: Profile of a City 312–1308.* 2nd rev. ed. Princeton: Princeton University Press, 1980.

Kuttner, Stephan. "Cardinalis: The History of a Canonical Concept." *Traditio* 3 (1943): 149–50.

———. "Universal Pope or Servant of God's Servants: The canonists, papal titles, and Innocent III." *Revue de droit canonique* 32 (1981): 109–23.

Kuttner, Stephan, and Antonio Garcia y Garcia. "A New Eyewitness Account of the Fourth Lateran Council. *Traditio* 20 (1964): 113–78.

Ladner, Gerhart B. *The Idea of Reform: Its Impact on Christian Thought and Action in the Age of the Fathers.* Cambridge, MA: Harvard University Press, 1959.

Lambert, Malcolm. *The Cathars (Peoples of Europe).* Malden, MN: Blackwell, 1998.

Lanham, Carol Dana. "Salutation Formulas in Latin Letters to 1200: Syntax, Style, and Theory." *Münchener Beiträge zur Mediavistik und Renaissance-Forschung* 22. München: Stefan Schwarz, 1975.

Latham, James E. *The Religious Symbolism of Salt.* Paris: Beauchesne, 1982.

Latham, R. E. *Revised Medieval Latin Word List from British and Irish Sources.* London, The British Academy: Oxford University Press, 1973.

*A Latin Dictionary.* Revised and expanded by Charlton T. Lewis. Oxford: Clarendon, 1980.

Leclercq, Jean. *Monks on Marriage: A Twelfth Century View.* New York: The Seabury Press, 1983.

Maccarrone, Michele. "The 'Chair of St. Peter' in the Middle Ages: from Symbol to Relic." In *Romana Ecclesia Cathedra Petri*. Ed. Piero Zerbi et al., vol. 2. Rome: Herder, 1991:1249–1373.

Maccarrone, Michele, et al. "Memorie," in *Atti Della Pontifica Accademia Romana Archeologia*, Serie III, 21. Rome: Tipografia Poliglotta Vaticana, 1971).

Maccarrone, Michele. *Vicarius Christi: Storia del Titolo Papale*. Rome: Facultas Theologica Pontificii Athenaei Lateranensis, 1952.

Maleczek, Werner. *Papst und Kardinalskolleg von 1191 bis 1216*. Vienna: Verlag der Osterreichischen Akademie der Wissenschaften, 1984.

*Mediae Latinitatis Lexicon Minus*. Comp. J. F. Niermeyer. Leiden: E. J. Brill, 1976.

J. P. Migne, ed. *Patrologiae Cursus Completus Series Latina*, 222 vols. Turnhout: Brepols, Reprint 1958.

Milgrom, Jacob. *Leviticus 1–16: A New Translation with Introduction and Commentary*. The Anchor Bible. New York: Doubleday, 1991.

Moore, I. R. *The Formation of a Persecuting Society: Power and Deviance in Western Europe, 950–1250*. Malden, MN: Blackwell, 1991.

Moore, John C. "Innocent III's 'De Miseria Humanae Conditionis': A Speculum Curiae?" *Catholic Historical Review* 67 (1981): 553–64.

Moore, John C. "The Sermons of Pope Innocent III." *Römische Historische Mitteilungen* 36 (1994): 82–142.

Morris, Colin. *The Papal Monarchy: The Western Church from 1050 to 1250*. Oxford: Clarendon, 1989.

Moynihan, James M. *Papal Immunity and Liability in the Writings of the Medieval Canonists*. Rome: Gregorian University Press, 1961.

Multhauf, Robert P. *Neptune's Gift: A History of Common Salt*. Baltimore: Johns Hopkins, 1978.

Munk, Connie Mae. *A Study of Pope Innocent III's Treatise: "De quadripartita specie nuptiarum."* 2 vols. Ph.D. dissertation, University of Kansas. Ann Arbor, Michigan: University Microfilms, 1975.

Munro, Dana C. "The Children's Crusade." *American Historical Review* 19 (1914): 516–24.

Murphy, James J. *Rhetoric in the Middle Ages: A History of Rhetorical Theory from Saint Augustine to the Renaissance*. Berkeley: University of California Press, 1974.

*The New Jerusalem Bible*. Ed. Henry Wansbrough et al. Garden City, NY: Doubleday, 1985.

Origen. *Selecta in Ezechielem*. PG 13.

*Oxford Dictionary of the Christian Church*. 2nd ed. Oxford University Press, 1974.

Pennington, Kenneth. "The Legal Education of Pope Innocent III" and "Innocent III's Knowledge of Law," both reprinted in *Popes, Canonists and Texts, 1150–1550*. Brookfield, Vermont: Variorum, 1993.

———. *Pope and Bishops: The Papal Monarchy in the Twelfth and Thirteenth Centuries.* University of Pennsylvania Press, 1984.

———. Review of Imkamp, *Kirchenbild*, in *Zeitschrift der Savigny-Stiftung für Rechtsgeschichte* 72 (1986): 417–28.

Peter of Blois. *Sermons*. PL 207.

Peter the Chanter. *Verbum Abbreviatum.* PL 205.

Peter Lombard. *Commentarium in Psalmos.* PL 191.

*The Peterborough Chronicle.* Rev. ed. Ed. Cecily Clark. Oxford: Clarendon Press, 1970.

Peters, Edward. *Inquisition.* New York: The Free Press, 1988.

Pope, Marvin H. *Song of Songs: A New Translation with Introduction and Commentary,* The Anchor Bible. Garden City, NY, Doubleday, 1977.

Post, Gaines. "Copyists' Errors and the Problem of Papal Dispensations 'Contra Statutum Generale Ecclesiae' or 'Contra Statum Generalem Ecclesiae' According to the Decretists and Decretalists ca. 1150–1234." *Studia Gratiana* 9 (1966): 357–405.

Powell, James M., ed. *Innocent III: Vicar of Christ or Lord of the World?* 2nd exp. Washington, D.C.: The Catholic University of America Press, 1994.

Rabanus Maurus. *De clericorum instructione.* PL 107.

Rahner, Karl. *Bishops: Status and Function.* Trans. Edward Quinn. Baltimore: Helicon Press, 1964.

Roberts, Phyllis B. "The Pope and the Preachers: Perceptions of the Religious Role of the Papacy in the Preaching Tradition of the Thirteenth-Century English Church." In *Religious Roles of the Papacy: Ideals and Realities, 1150–1300.* Ed. Christopher Ryan. Toronto: Pontifical Institute of Mediaeval Studies, 1989.

———. *Stephanus de Lingua-Tonante: Studies in the Sermons of Stephen Langton.* Toronto: Pontifical Institute of Mediaeval Studies, 1968.

Schimmelpfennig, Bernhard. *The Papacy.* Trans. James Sievert. New York: Columbia University Press, 1992.

Scuppa, Giuseppe. *I Sermoni di Innocenzo III.* Rome: masch. diss., Pontificia Universitas Lateranensis, 1961.

Skeehand, Patrick W., and Alexander A. Di Lella. *The Wisdom of Ben Sira.* The Anchor Bible. New York: Doubleday, 1987.

Smalley, Beryl. *The Study of the Bible in the Middle Ages.* Notre Dame, IN: University of Notre Dame Press, 1964.

Stickler, Alfons M. "Papal Infallibility—a Thirteenth Century Invention? Reflections on a Recent Book." *The Catholic Historical Review* 70 (1974): 427–41.

Synan, Edward A. "The Pope's 'Other Sheep.'" In *Religious Roles of the Papacy: Ideals and Realities, 1150–1300.* Ed. Christopher Ryan. Toronto: Pontifical Institute of Mediaeval Studies, 1989.

*Synodi Sinuessanae de Marcellino papa.* PL 6.

Tanner, Norman P., ed. *Decrees of the Ecumenical Councils.* 2 vols. Original text established by G. Alberigo et al. New York and Washington, D.C.: Sheed and Ward with Georgetown University Press, 1990.

Tierney, Brian. *Foundations of Conciliar Theory: The Contribution of the Medieval Canonists from Gratian to the Great Schism.* Cambridge: Cambridge University Press, 1955.

Tierney, Brian. *Origins of Papal Infallibility 1150–1350: A Study on the Concepts of Infallibility, Sovereignty and Tradition in the Middle Ages.* Leiden: E. J. Brill, 1972.

Tillmann, Helene. *Pope Innocent III.* Trans. Walter Sax. New York: North-Holland Publishing Co., 1980.

Trexler, Richard C. *The Christian at Prayer: an Illustrated Prayer Manual Attributed to Peter the*

*Chanter (d. 1197).* Medieval and Renaissance Texts & Studies. Binghamton, NY, 1987.

Ullman, Walter. "Innocent III." *New Catholic Encyclopedia.* Washington, D.C.: The Catholic University of America and McGraw Hill Book Company, 1967.

Van Dijk, Stephen J. T., and Joan Hazelden Walker. *The Ordinal of the Papal Court from Innocent III to Boniface VIII and Related Documents.* Fribourg: University Press, 1975.

Vorreux, Damien. *Un Symbole Franciscan: Le Tau.* Paris: Editions Franciscaines, 1977.

Watkins, Oscar D. *A History of Penance: Being a Study of the Authorities.* 2 vols. London: Longmans, Green, 1920.

Watt, James A. *The Theory of Papal Monarchy in the Thirteenth Century: the Contribution of the Canonists.* New York: Fordham University Press, 1965.

William of Conches. *Glossae super platonem.* Ed. Edouard Jeanneau. Paris: Vrin, 1965.

Willibald. "Life of St. Boniface," in *Anglo-Saxon Missionaries in Germany.* Trans. C. H. Talbot. New York: Sheed and Ward, 1954.

# INDEX OF MODERN AUTHORS

# SCRIPTURAL INDEX

*Between God and Man: Six Sermons on the Priestly Office* was designed and composed in Centaur by Kachergis Book Design, Pittsboro, North Carolina; and printed on 60-pound Glatfelter and bound by Cushing-Malloy, Inc., Ann Arbor, Michigan.